Moments of
Redemption

Moments of Redemption

Cover Photo and Photo Editing: M. Roc Pe'rine for -MRocArt- a Centcom Entertainment Company LLC (www.centcoment.net)

Makeup: Brianna Thompson

Editor: Chaun Johnson

This book is a memoir. Some names and identifying details have been changed to protect the privacy of individuals.

ISBN: 978-1-089-30124-0

Printed in the United States of America

Dedication

The decision to write a book, especially one as personal as this one, is not an easy decision. In fact, it is downright terrifying because while I am telling my story it lays bare who I am, but it also exposes the people around me, especially my family. Therefore, this is not just a book about me, it is about my corner of the world, my experiences, and how they have made me the woman, mother, spouse, daughter, granddaughter, sister, and friend I am today.

This is not a book written because I believe I am more important than anyone else or that my story bears more weight than the next person. On the contrary, it is written because I think my journey and my experience, is not that unusual, in both good ways and bad. I think the journey my life took, and continues to take, is important, not because of me, but because it is relatable and recognizable. My story has lessons that are worth sharing in the hopes it will assist others in seeing themselves and maybe give them the strength in knowing they are not alone. Ultimately it is a book about relationships, both romantic and otherwise. It is a candid look behind my curtain and the mask I display at times to uncover the lessons that I have learned and perhaps the lessons the person reading this may have learned or is currently learning. No one makes it through life unscathed when it comes to relationships. We're all going to make mistakes, make the wrong choices, and get our hearts broken occasionally.

And if we are honest with ourselves, some of those times we are the cause of the heartache.

I thank God for giving me the vision, and the strength, to publicly share my story. For many years I lived an extremely private life. But I learned there is just as much damage in saying too little as there is in saying too much. Some of my life events were for me and others were for the people in my midst. But my healing always came when I became courageous enough to share my story. My testimony is the conduit that always ushers me from tragedy to triumph. And I thank God for being so patient with me as I am still a work in progress.

This memoir is dedicated to my faithful family. Thank you for offering unwavering encouragement and support when I need it most. You inspire me and every step I take is with you in mind. I love you all very deeply. I hope that what I share in here is seen through the lens of love that it was written in, no matter how difficult the words and realities may appear in black and white. This is about my journey. But it is a journey that was impossible without a lot of people. I hope this book makes you proud.

"There is no love without forgiveness, and there is no forgiveness without love."
- Bryant H. McGill

Table of Content

CHAPTER
One

The Makings of Me

or most of my life, I have trusted no one, assumed the worse in people and feared being abandoned by those that meant the most to me. I spent much of my adulthood attempting to tame my quick temper, curtail my controlling ways, and suppress a burning desire for validation in romantic relationships and extramarital affairs. Most therapists and life coaches would likely describe me as "broken." But everyone has a back story. Let me tell you mine!

When I was six years old my mother met and fell in love with a charismatic country man from Louisiana named William. The two began their yearlong courtship after meeting through mutual friends one afternoon at work. William introduced himself as a hardworking southern gentleman who had recently moved to the area in pursuit of a more promising career. Will was focused on establishing himself in a new city and building his career. He seemed like a great catch. And as he captured the attention of my mother, he also won my innocent heart.

Will entered our lives at a critical point in time. The year was 1988, and I was entering the first grade at one of the area's most prominent Catholic schools. At the same time, my mother was excelling in her career at a national telecommunications firm. Mom was admired by her company as a devoted employee with the promise of a bright future. She was the picture-perfect woman to settle down with and Will seemed like the ideal man.

Months later, the two married and we began our lives as a blended family. Will embraced me as his daughter and proudly introduced me to his friends and family as "his baby girl". He presented me to the world like a jeweler offers a precious gem. We spent lots of quality time together often bonding over sports. If we were not on the basketball court working on my left-handed crossover, we were yelling at the opinionated commentators on the Saturday morning ESPN shows. With the absence of my biological father, Will seemed to be an ideal father figure. But reality always supersedes appearance.

The truth was, Will married my mom and took on a "readymade family" without thoroughly understanding what the role entailed. Prior to doing so, he saw few examples of marriage and he had not been exposed to any positive male role models. In no time, it seemed like Will transformed from a great catch to a horrible husband. My mom later discovered that Will struggled with drugs and alcohol and was both physically and emotionally abusive. He lost the job that they originally met at and often bounced from one low paying job to another during his brief stints of employment. It quickly became evident that Will presented himself as one thing but showed up to the marriage as something else. He was content with being unemployed and allowing my mother to shoulder the responsibility of caring for our family.

Childhood memories can sometimes be tricky. There are those moments in your life that fade away as if they never happened. But then there are those memories etched into your psyche as if they occurred hours prior. One memory that is imprinted into the depths of my soul is one of my stepfather hitting, punching and kicking my mother as she lay helplessly at his feet.

This Sunday afternoon began like most others had in the past. My mother and I prepared to make our way to my grandparents' house for dinner. Sunday dinner was always a weekly tradition in my family that is rooted in our culture's embrace of good food, fun and family fellowship. As my mother arose from her comfortable spot next to Will on the couch, she called me from my room and instructed me to put my shoes on so that we could head out of the door. We prepared to leave the apartment when my mother turned and extended one last offer for Will to join us. After little consideration, he declined her offer slumping deeper into the couch. With no hesitation we walked out of the apartment continuing our journey to my grandparent's house.

When mom and I arrived, no one expected to see my stepdad. Will and my grandfather did not get along and my grandfather made it clear that he did not feel that Will was good enough for his daughter. My grandfather was a man's man. He believed that a man that did not work did not eat. He would say that a man's role in his family was to protect, profess and provide for himself, his mate and his legacy. He hated the notion of my mother working more than Will but was especially unhappy with my mother carrying the family and Will's unborn child at the same time.

It was a warm sunny evening when we headed back home to the Preston Heights Apartments in Joliet. My mother pulled into the parking lot and parked her black 1993 Hyundai Elantra in her assigned parking spot. We grabbed our leftovers from dinner, locked the car doors and walked down the sidewalk past the playing children that were drawing on the sidewalk with the large sticks of chalk. I trailed behind my mom like a baby duck as she climbed the six stairs leading to the outer door of this large brick building. It was good to be home, but this indeed was a change from the solidarity of my grandparent's tranquil neighborhood. As we entered the outer door of the building my mom turned around and looked at me.

"Candy, did you grab the food from out the car?" she asked.

"Yes, I got it Mommy," I replied.

I watched her as she walked in front of me. My mommy was the cutest pregnant woman that I had ever seen. My mom not only favored my grandfather but also embodied his charismatic ways. She was confident, fun, and could light up a room when she entered. She was the life of the party. Looking at her in this moment, on that day, it was slightly comical because she was all legs and stomach as we awaited the arrival of my sibling.

When we entered the apartment, Will was sitting on the couch in front of the television. He had returned to his original seat from earlier. But I remember the faint smell of fish. His fishing cooler was set neatly in the corner of the kitchen next to the wall. I knew this meant that he had just returned from one of his fishing trips. As he stared off at the commercial on television, he looked like a giant on the small couch. He was a brown skinned man, with a muscular build standing at about 5'10". He was wearing a pair of light denim jeans, a 49ers t-shirt, and a pair of black Converse gym shoes. My mom greeted him and proceeded to the kitchen to store the plate she had brought for him to eat in the refrigerator.

"Will, I brought you something to eat." She called from the kitchen.

After greeting my stepfather, I continued past the living room to my bedroom so I could play with my toys. A few minutes later I started to hear escalating commotion coming from the living room. Will's voice quickly began to rise, and I immediately became concerned. Stepping out of my bedroom to investigate what was going on I was met with my stepfather standing close to my mom and yelling at her. I could not understand what was going on because this was the first time, I had witnessed such an altercation between them. I stood there frozen trying to understand what I was seeing with my seven-year-old mind.

"Would you stop! Don't do this in front of Candy. You're scaring her." my mom exclaimed.

I had not shown any emotion or expressed that I was afraid so I believe she was deflecting her feelings on me in hopes this would cause him to calm down. This scene was so out of character for him and once I grew older, I realized that this was because he was likely under the influence of alcohol, drugs or both.

Watching this scene, I saw my strong, independent mom diminish in his very presence. It seemed like the more he yelled and the more enraged he became the demurer she converted. My mother retreated into the bedroom with the hopes of deescalating the situation. Feeling a slight level of relief, I believed my mom and my unborn sibling would be safe and my stepfather would return to the couch and continue watching television.

Unfortunately, this was not the case. My stepfather followed my mother into the bedroom and the door closed behind him. Standing there in disbelief and wanting to go to my mom I had no clue as to what I should be doing in that moment. Suddenly I began to hear the disturbing sound of slapping and my mother began to scream out to me.

"Candy, run to your auntie's house! Go now!" she yelled.

My aunt lived in an adjacent building across the parking lot from our building. I wasted no time running from our second-floor apartment, down the hallway, and out of our building. The world looked different than it had moments ago when I was reveling over my adorable pregnant mom. I was not concerned about the guys hanging around in the parking lot, the kids playing at the playground, or the cars that were making their way through the complex. The only thing I could think about was getting help for my mom who when I escaped the apartment with the slight fish smell was being slapped behind a closed door.

The few yards to my aunt's building seemed like miles but when I made it, I laid on the buzzer pleading for her or one of my cousins to answer the door. I pressed and pressed and pressed. It seemed like hours before my aunt answered and buzzed me in. I broke through the door, ran up to the third floor, and into my aunt's apartment.

"Candy, what is it?" she exclaimed when she saw my disheveled and panicked appearance.

"Call the police, he's hitting her! He's hitting my mom!" I screamed.

"Who?"

"Will. He got so mad."

Before I could explain any further my aunt had dialed 911, told me to stay there in her apartment, grabbed her keys and sprinted from her unit. I raced to the window to see if I could see what was happening, but her apartment faced the opposite direction. I could not stand being in there alone and all I knew is I wanted my mom. I ran from my aunt's apartment and when I emerged from her building, I could see the fight had made its way out into the parking lot.

I saw my mom trying to flee from the building and my stepdad close behind her trying to drag her back into the building. The guys who were previously minding their own business and talking were now gaping at the scene unfolding in front of their eyes. I could see women peeking out the windows trying to see what the commotion was about. The kids in the playground came to a pause and were pointing, talking, and some laughing. But with all the onlookers present, no one attempted to go to my mom's rescue. No one tried to help my aunt in restraining my stepfather's attack.

My mom was able to break free and made it far enough away to lay down in the grass near the playground in a fetal position with the hopes of protecting her unborn child. Still no one came to her rescue. I ran to my mom hoping to comfort her as I heard the sirens of the police approaching. I kneeled next to her with tears quietly falling down my cheeks wondering how this could have happened. Was she going to be ok? And had I done the best I could to protect her?

The next moments went quickly. When the police arrived, they called for an ambulance because it was evident my mother needed medical attention. Everyone was disbursed in different directions. My stepfather was taken away by the police, my mom was taken away by ambulance, and I was taken to my grandparent's house.

My mother spent several days in the hospital. I had questions for my grandparents that went unanswered. I am sure it was for my protection and there are just some things that children did not need to know. The first night that I stayed over, I asked if I could go to wherever my mom was. By the next night I laid in bed crying for mommy. As I laid there with tears streaming down my cheeks, I stared out of the window looking at the twinkling stars of the summer sky asking God to watch over her. I begged God to fix whatever mess had been made. I offered to be a better little girl if He did this one favor for me. I would listen more, eat my veggies and clean up without being asked to do so. I had nothing to offer but my heart and I prayed to God as if my life depended on it. The thought of seeing my mom like that broke my heart. I had no words and saw images of the incident every time I closed my eyes to go to sleep. How could someone who said that they love you hurt you like this? I was sad, afraid, alone and uncertain about what the future would hold. I had more questions than answers and the adults often stopped speaking whenever I entered a room in the house. They worked diligently to protect what innocence remained.

The day finally came when I was taken to visit my mom in the hospital. As I walked into the large, cold, sterile building I wondered if my mom was lonely in here. I walked just inches from the heels of my Granny's white Reebok gym shoes as I observed doctors and nurses passing by tending to their duties. No one paying us any specific attention as we made our way to the bank of elevators adjacent to the Main Level Giftshop. We pressed five and road in silence to our desired floor. As we exited the elevator, I can still recall the varying sounds of little babies crying. The scent of Johnson & Johnson lotion made its way into my nose as we passed some of the rooms. As we continued walking down the hallway the atmosphere shifted from jovial celebration, well-lit rooms with families and balloons, and little bassinets carrying their tiny passengers to a corridor that was much quieter, dimly lit, and void of bassinets, balloons, or little cries.

We arrived at a closed door and stopped for a moment. My grandmother looked deep into my eyes for what seemed like an eternity. I reached for her hand and she squeezed it for reassurance and without uttering a word, she transferred the courage and tenacity that I needed to walk through that door. As we pressed the silver handle, the door creaked open. The room was dark as my Mom laid still in a fetal position in the center of the partially raised hospital bed. My Granny called out to my mom jolting her attention towards us as we approached her bedside. I walked over to my mom's bed and she sat up shifting the overhead light to the on position. She gazed at me and smiled. I cannot recall the exact words that were spoken in this moment. But I glanced around the room taking inventory of all that I saw. I saw no little bassinet carrying a little passenger. There was no scent of baby lotion. And my mom's stomach was smaller than I had seen in months. Even at the age of seven, something in me knew not to inquire about the sibling that we spoke so much about. Because I knew when my mom was able to leave the hospital she would be leaving alone.

This incident is one that is never discussed in my family. But I found it to be the inspiration of one of the most important lessons that I learned about life, love, and the pursuit of romantic happiness. In life I believe we all show up to new relationships with baggage. We dress up the best version of ourselves and present it to a prospective partner. We eventually fall in love; life happens and at some point, the real work begins. It is in the crux of the relationship that our true layers of brokenness are exposed, and we begin to see one another for the true individuals that we always were. As I have reflected on this incident, I often wanted to blame my stepfather for being a bad person and a disappointment to my mother and me. Then I wanted to blame his drug and alcohol abuse for being the disease that kept him from being the best version of himself that he could have been. Yet, as I have grown and experienced life myself, I came to the realization that it was so much more than just placing a label on him and calling him a bad person. I have learned that in many ways we are simply a reflection of those things we have experienced and witnessed as we have gone on our journey of life. I would often grapple with the notion that maybe his actions were due to his lack of male role models or father figures. From stories that I learned over the years, I realized he did not know how to be a husband because he had never seen a husband. None of these things are meant to be excuses or a way to reason why my mother endured some of the things she did. But it does make me realize that for every poor decision, negative action, or flawed character trait one possesses, there is usually a back story that molded the person to be who they show up to be.

"The decisions made in life and love are the direct reflections of the examples modeled before us. Most people run to or from those feelings that are true or familiar."

- Candy

CHAPTER

Two

Letting Go

As I continued to travel through life one thing that continued, which I had no control over, was the fact that my suitcase was continuing to grow. We all have a suitcase that travels through life with us whether we choose to acknowledge it or not. These suitcases can stem from emotional, spiritual, and physical hurts, traumas, and disappointments. For some that suitcase is light. For some it is extremely heavy and you must pay the oversize charge to carry it with you. And still for some they must carry multiple suitcases. No matter which category you fall in, we all have baggage that at some point has to be unpacked.

Unzipping my largest suitcase would reveal mounds of misplaced aggression and an inability to express my emotions. During my childhood, I witnessed some unhealthy tactics on how conflict in relationships was resolved. As I made my way into the world of relationships and dating, I saw evidence of this manifesting itself in my first serious relationship.

In January 2002, I arrived as an incoming freshman on the campus of Illinois State University. Nicole was the first person I met that Monday morning as I walked into the classroom and took my seat in the back of the room. This once in a lifetime meeting was a pivotal moment in some events that later occurred in my life. I had no idea as I sat sneaking glances at this beautiful woman as the professor rambled on about the syllabus and what was to come during this Spring semester that this was the beginning of a three year long emotional rollercoaster.

When we were dismissed from class, I grabbed my messenger bag, coat, scarf, and hat and made my way towards the front of the class to leave. I passed by Nicole as she was gathering her things and stole one last glance without her knowledge before making my way out to the hallway. As I made my way to the elevator, I was thinking at least I'll have something pretty to look at during those moments my fleeting attention span takes me away from the lecture at hand.

"Hey you. Wait a minute!" I heard a voice calling behind me.

I turned around to find Nicole racing towards me trying to get my attention. I slowed down so I could determine if she was truly trying to get my attention or perhaps the attention of someone else.

"Sorry. I didn't mean to call you "you" but I didn't catch your name in the class." she said.

I stood there for a few seconds surprised she was trying to get my attention. She stood there about 5'8" with a beautiful brown complexion devoid of any makeup. She had beautiful dark brown eyes and an infectious smile. I was instantly drawn in. If I was Earth, she was my gravitational pull.

"So, can I have your name?" she said pulling me back into the present.

"Sure. My friends call me Candy. What's yours?" I responded.

"Nicole. Do you have another class after this?" she probed.

I thought for a moment trying to recall my schedule in my mind. "No. I'm done for the day."

"You want to go grab something to eat? I'm starving." she smiled.

"Sure."

I accepted the invite without hesitation considering I was brand new to the campus and had not had the opportunity to meet many people other than the girls on my floor in my dorm. We went to one of the campus diners in Watterson Towers and grabbed some food using our meal plans that was so graciously loaded onto our school IDs. Over lunch we enjoyed conversation which included us exchanging our stories on where we were from, how long we had been at the school, and what dorm we stayed in.

I learned that Nicole had also just started during this Spring semester rather than the prior Fall semester because she had served in the Navy and was just starting her collegiate career. In just that short lunch I learned Nicole was more than just a beautiful face but had traveled the world and was one of the most intelligent women that you could ever meet. She appeared to have a plan and knew what she wanted to accomplish from day one. She shared with me that her plan was to graduate with her bachelor's degree in political science and attend law school. I was intrigued.

After lunch it was evident, we were not ready to part ways. We ended up going bowling at the campus Bowling and Billiards Center followed by dinner. While bowling I learned how she had traveled the world and she let me in on some of her military moments. Over dinner the conversation flowed effortlessly. Before I knew it, I was standing in Nicole's dorm room watching her pack an overnight bag so we could return to my room to retire for the night. That night we explored one another physically as well as mentally. From the first kiss we could never keep our hands off each other. The physical attraction was magnetic.

When she finally left my room the next afternoon I was left with my thoughts and relishing in what my first day away at college had brought my way. Was this love at first sight? There was something so intense and mysterious about my connection to Nicole. It was certainly way more than what I thought I had with my high school sweetheart. We had been immediately drawn to one another. It was as if our chance meeting was serendipitous. From that day forward Nicole had me. My nose was officially wide open for her and what was to come sent me through a tailspin to say the least. In that relationship I experienced things I had never experienced before and some things I never did again.

Over the course of the semester we would literally spend every day together. When you saw Candy, you saw Nicole, and vice versa. I fell deeply for her and had no problem professing my love for her and to her. I wanted to be with her and make her the happiest woman in the world. We continued our relationship until the end of the school year. Summer break approached, and it was time to move out of our dorms and return home for the summer. I was heartbroken to see her go. The few months apart would prove to be the turning point in our relationship. She immediately returned home and began spending time with an old friend known through Chicago as Cashmere. Although I had reservations about their friendship, I never expressed them to Nicole. I never wanted her to think that I was the jealous or insecure type. I never wanted my small suitcase at the time to mistakenly pop open and expose the baggage I had already carried into our new and budding relationship.

The summer months drug on and the time for us to return to school was approaching. I could not wait because I was ready to get back to our daily routine of spending time with one another, sleeping next to each other, and nurturing the bond we were forming. One August morning, I received a call on my cell phone. It quickened me from my sleep and I had to hurry to silence the alarm before it disturbed my mother. Looking at the display I saw it was Nicole and I also observed the time. It was nearly two a.m.

I gathered myself and answered groggily, "Hey baby. What's wrong?"

I knew something had to be awry because we had already spoke that evening and said our goodnights to one another until the next day. Nicole was screaming and crying hysterically. I could barely make out what was being said.

"He raped me! He raped me!" she exclaimed.

I immediately sat up in the bed. My heart was racing and I worked to try to calm her down so I could determine what had happened and where she was. She mustered up the strength to be able to describe to me the events as they had unfolded. She explained that she was with Cashmere earlier in the evening. She stated that Cashmere, his roommate, and several other friends hosted a dinner party at his downtown Chicago loft. She explained that everyone was eating and drinking and having a great time when Cashmere asked to speak with her privately. He said he had something he wanted to talk to her about and did not want to have to yell over the loud music that everyone was now dancing to. He escorted her into his bedroom, closed and locked the door, and before she could ascertain what was about to happen, he began to rape her. She explained that she told him that the advances were not wanted, screamed no, cried and attempted to fight him off.

She said I had been the first person she called after being home for hours. Scared, hurt, and disgusted, she stated that she never called the police, never told anyone and was uncertain on what to do. I did not know what to make of this. I was young, naïve and completely conflicted in how I felt. I wanted to believe my girlfriend but there were some elements of the story that simply did not make any sense. But how can you say anything like that when someone has just reached out to you in a state of hysteria and provided this horrific account.

I spent the next few weeks trying to convince her to call the police or tell someone.

"You can't just let this go. He raped you!" I said to her.

"But what should I do? Who should I tell?" she would respond.

"Call the police. He can't just do this to people and be able to walk away." I retorted.

"It's ok. I don't talk to him anymore and I just want to put it behind me."

This conversation occurred multiple times with no results. At eighteen years old, I could not wrap my mind around how someone could be violated and not say anything. As I grew older, I heard the stories of victims and understood better how some can go for a long time without saying anything, if at all.

One day shortly before we were preparing to head back to campus Nicole calls me. When I answered there was something in her voice that was unsettling. She had a petrified tone and was speaking very softly on the phone.

"What's going on?" I asked.

"I need you to come see me as soon as you can. We need to talk" she insisted.

I climbed into my 1989 Pontiac Grand Prix and made my way down I-80 East towards Chicago. I made my way to her mother's house on 71st and Lowe on the Southside, picked her up, and rented a hotel room. It was at that moment that I wanted to be able to look her in the eye and ask her some serious questions after hearing what she had to say. I had been uneasy for weeks and I wanted to get everything cleared up before we made our way back to campus. I had to know if the story she had told me weeks prior was real or fake.

She stood quietly behind me as we stood at the hotel counter checking in. I made light conversation with the front desk clerk and obtained our key.

"Thank you so much ladies. You two have a good night and feel free to call down if you need anything." the clerk said.

"Okay. Thanks." I replied.

I made my way to the room and slid the room door key into the black box and waited for the green light to illuminate giving me permission to access our home for the night. I saw the light and heard the soft click of the door unlocking and opened it. I held the door and stepped to the side to allow Nicole to walk in first like I always did. We placed our bags on the desk in the room and I sat down in the little office chair. Nicole sat down on the bed in front of me. She avoided making eye contact with me and I knew then this night was probably not going to go the way our nights usually went.

"Baby look at me. What's wrong? What's going on?" I quizzed.

She looked up at me and tears started to slowly roll down her cheeks. It felt like hours passed before the words escaped her lips that would completely alter my life. I was unprepared for what I was about to learn.

"I'm pregnant."

I looked at her with eyes glossed over with confusion. I never would have imagined how those two words could literally take my breath away and make me feel like I was about to pass out. Over the next several hours she cried and pleaded with me. She desperately wanted our committed relationship to continue. She said she needed my love and support through this and that she loved me. What did she really want from me? I was an 18-year-old college student waiting to enter my second semester. I had not even started my life yet. What could I offer her or a child that I never planned to have? And for that matter, a child she claimed she had not planned for.

Some say that love is blind. I would argue that for a teenager, love is being stupid or making stupid choices. I became a fool for Nicole. After that night I made the choice to continue the relationship and I was all in. We made the decision that when we returned to campus, we were going to tell everyone the baby was planned. We had to keep up the image of being the "it couple" and of course Nicole did not want to let anyone know of the rape. After all, I loved her and I wanted to marry her one day.

We finished out the remainder of the summer and then made our way back to Normal, IL. Because we had to now plan for a baby I had to scramble and make some major adjustments. Instead of two dorm rooms, I had found us a two-bedroom townhouse near campus. I found a job working for the hospital near campus full time while also attending school on a full-time basis. The Grand Prix was traded in for a 2001 Chrysler Sebring. I wanted her to be comfortable and I did not want her to worry about anything but going to class and taking care of herself and our growing baby.

By the following February, the baby had arrived. Although I never envisioned myself as a parent this young, I was in love and welcomed Nicole's daughter into the world as my own. I even signed the birth certificate and gave her my last name. For the next year and a half, we were a happy family unit. We took family pictures, took family trips, and spent the holidays with family. We had even moved into a larger apartment that was one story for the baby's safety.

But, as I learned through my childhood experiences, nothing remained perfect and the moment came where the true tests of love, patience, and forgiveness came our way. There was a major shift that came over our relationship. My loving attentive girlfriend began to act cold and withdrawn. I thought this was due to the long hours that I worked at the hospital or the hours of schoolwork and class that I put in each week. Perhaps she was feeling overwhelmed with caring for the baby or felt lonely. I was big on communication so I never allowed anything to go too long without addressing it. We talked about the issues but nothing was ever resolved.

Amid everything I had going on I had met a girl at Chatters, one of the campus dining halls I visited between classes. While sitting alone, as I often did, enjoying my lunch, I felt someone standing over me. I looked up and there was a thin, modestly dressed, dark skinned girl with dreads.

"Hi. I'm Kendall." she said as she extended her hand.

A little puzzled, I returned the gesture. Who was she and what did she want?

"I'm Candy."

"Sorry to bother you. But I noticed your ribbon. I'm hoping I'm not interrupting you." she said referencing the rainbow ribbon that I proudly displayed on my messenger bag.

"No bother. Did you need something?" I quizzed.

"Well, I'm new here and you looked like someone nice."

I chuckled a little bit at what she was saying and at the plain black slacks and pale button up shirt she was wearing as if she was on her way to a campus job interview. She seemed cool so I invited her to join me at the table. We sat and talked as I finished my lunch and she shared she was from North Carolina and was currently pursuing her master's degree in Social Work. There was a group on campus called Pride for those that identify with the LGBTQIA community. Kendall asked me if I was an active member with them because she had been looking into it along with some of the other African American groups on campus. I told her I knew about Pride and had attended a couple of their events but I was not an active member. Before going our separate ways, we exchanged numbers and I let her know I would keep her updated on any events I knew about that she may be interested in.

Later that evening I returned home to my woman and little one. I told Nicole about Kendall and she said she appeared to be interesting. Over time, Kendall and I kept in touch from time to time. The communication between her and I began to be more frequent. She expressed interest in developing new friendships with likeminded intelligent ladies in the gay and lesbian community. During this time there was a telltale sign that I either ignored or was too blind to see. Nicole would ask me about Kendall and then she kept encouraging me to invite her over for dinner. Being none the wiser I obliged.

The night Kendall came for dinner, it appeared to go smoothly. We had some mutual friends over to introduce Kendall to other ladies in the hopes she would be able to foster some additional connections. We all sat around talking and exchanging stories. As the night progressed, the crowd began to dissipate leaving only Kendall behind. I can recall leaving the room to tend to the baby leaving Nicole and Kendall alone. Thinking back on things, that was probably the moment it all started. The slow descent to hell was thrust into motion that night.

Over the months that followed it seemed my new acquaintance was beginning to interweave herself deeper into my existence. She made her appearance at the church Nicole and I attended after asking if we had a church home. She quickly transitioned from a visitor to a member. She would make a point to approach us after service every week. She always found a way to pull something from the service to have a fleeting conversation with Nicole before we made our departure. Observing their mannerisms with one another over the next several weeks my suspicions began to rise that there may be a little more than just weekly church banter between my woman and my so-called acquaintance.

"You guys seem to be getting kind of close." I said as I drove us home from church.

"Who?" Nicole responded in a curious manner.

I responded with just one word, "Kendall."

"Candy really? I was just saying hi and talking about what Pastor said in his sermon today. Get a grip!" she retorted.

"Yeah. Ok." I said

As time pressed on, I became increasingly suspicious that they were having an affair. One day while I was at the hospital working, I got this overwhelming feeling that something was going on. So, I put my women's intuition to the test. I had always heard about women's intuition but thought it was just something women used as an excuse to be able to snoop around or blame their mate when they were not happy. On my lunch break I decided to call Nicole to see if I could detect anything that would explain the bad feeling I was having. Her conversation was extremely short which was out of character for her. Normally she would want to stay on the phone with me until my break was almost complete.

"Hey baby. What you doing?" I asked.

"Nothing. Playing with the baby. How's work?"

"It's going ok. I was missing you guys." I said.

"Oh ok. Well I have to go. I'll see you tonight when you get home."

I immediately heard the phone click before I had the opportunity to say anything else or even properly end the conversation. The conversation left me angry and uneasy. I went to my supervisor and made up an excuse so I could end my shift early to head home. I could not ignore the pitfall feeling I had in my stomach, the nausea, and the heat I felt on the tips of my ears from my rising anger. It is the oddest thing to be upset and not even truly have a reason to be mad. But there I was, pissed like I had just had a monstrous argument with someone.

As I made the drive back to the apartment that we shared there were multiple possibilities of what I might discover when I made it home. What if the two of them were together? What if I am wrong? What if I do not discover anything but still have the looming suspicion of infidelity...how do I continue in the relationship? The questions kept coming and I had no answers. The only thing I knew for certain was that I had to continue home and deal with whatever consequences may arise. I was completely in love with this woman and felt like I was begging her for what should have been given to me freely; honesty.

I sped down our street and as I grew closer to our apartment complex, I saw a car that looked familiar parked near one of the adjacent apartment buildings near ours. As I slowed to get a better look, I was able to verify it was Kendall's car. I assume she thought she was being clever and disguising her whereabouts should someone drive through the complex and spot her car. It was the worse job of hiding in plain sight.

As I parked my car and shut off the ignition my heart was beating out my chest. If anyone had seen the events that followed, they would have thought they were watching the sequel to Temptation by Tyler Perry. My breath was shallow, I was sweating, and breathing hard. My adrenalin was in high gear as I grabbed my keys and made sure my door key was ready to be used. I did not want to make any additional sounds or provide any extra time for the occupants inside to be able to camouflage anything that was going on.

As I entered the apartment it was quiet. The only sound I could hear in the distance was the television coming from the bedroom I shared with Nicole. As I quietly made my way down the hallway I peeked in the baby's room and could see she was fast asleep. I kissed her little forehead and for a moment I thought everything was ok and maybe I had been paranoid for no reason.

That feeling did not last long as I heard a soft moan come from the direction of my bedroom that sounded all too familiar. The hair stood up on the back of my neck. When I opened the bedroom door what I observed next had me seeing red. The glow from the television gave me just enough light to see the immense level of betrayal that was occurring in my bed. I saw the familiar landscape of Nicole's naked body that I always considered my playground. The second naked body was foreign but the love making was very familiar. To see activities being done that I thought were designated for only me made me lose control.

"WHAT THE FUCK!" I yelled.

Before I realized it, I was charging at them both and they scattered. Nicole scurried to put on her clothes. Kendall grabbed her clothes and keys that were placed neatly on the dresser quickly while trying to avoid contact with me. It was as if her clothes and keys were gathered in one place so if a quick exit or escape had to be done there would be no time lost on trying to locate a sock, bra, or any other random item of clothing.

"WHAT ARE YOU DOING HERE?" Nicole screamed.

"I FUCKING LIVE HERE. THE FUCK YOU MEAN?"

Nicole had diverted my attention long enough for Kendall to be able to flee from the apartment unscathed. That, of course, was not my intentions. Nicole and I continued arguing.

"Stop screaming before you wake up the baby." she snapped.

"Oh, now you're worried about waking up the baby. Are you serious right now?"

"Why are you acting like you are surprised by this?" she said.

I could not believe I had come home to this and Nicole was now treating me like she had never loved me. I quizzed her about what made her do it? Did she not love me anymore? Did I not treat her well? The more questions I asked, the more agitated Nicole appeared to become. We were both in tears after a while of arguing. My tears were from hurt, disappointment, and anger. I honestly could not say what hers were from.

She screamed and told me that the affair had been going on for a while. There were moments as we cried, screamed and argued that she would get close to me and I could smell the undeniable scent of sex permeating the air. Each time I smelled it my anger level rose until I eventually lost what was left of my mind. It was in that moment that I lost control and left my morals in the room in which we stood. I swung at Nicole and she swung back at me. I wanted the hurt and anger to stop and I had no idea of how to express the emotions that I felt.

It was then that I recalled everything I had sacrificed to be with her, support her, and care for a baby that I still was not a hundred percent certain was the product of rape. My family hated the idea of me being a lesbian ever since they found out when I was in high school. Because I chose her, I had not talked to them in months. They financially stopped assisting me which is why I was killing myself working full time and going to school full time. I was alone and lonely. Nicole and the baby were all I had in this world and in the twinkling of an eye it was all gone.

I am unsure how long we were fighting. I cannot recall when the baby started crying in the other room. Suddenly there was banging at our apartment door.

"POLICE! OPEN THE DOOR!" I heard from the other side of our front door.

Nicole ran into the room to calm the baby and I went to the door to answer for the police. There were three officers standing at the ready with their hands hovering over their guns when I opened the door. I could see two squad cars with their lights flashing drawing attention for all to see. Before I could get the door fully open, the officers rushed in.

"Can you tell us what is going on here? We received an anonymous call from someone in the area reporting a domestic disturbance." one of the officers barked at me.

"Nothing officer. We're fine." I said despite the scratches lightly bleeding on my neck and my t-shirt ripped in the back.

Nicole emerged carrying the baby looking just as disheveled as I was sans any bleeding wounds. The officers took one look at her with a crying baby in her arms and I knew deep down inside this was not going to go well. I was majoring in Criminal Justice after all and had observed the outcomes of many different cases involving domestic violence. Nicole was standing there the poster child for what a victim should look like with tears streaming down her face. Anonymous call my ass, I thought to myself, I know she called the police during one of the brief breaks in our fight. How dare she be the cause of this entire situation and then turn around and call the police on me.

The officers separated us and took our statements individually. Ten minutes later after collecting our statements one of the officers asked me to stand up and place my hands behind my back. I was being placed under arrest for battery. As I placed my hands behind my back and I felt the cold steel of the handcuffs wrap themselves around my wrist I looked up to see Nicole standing there.

"Can she bring me some shoes, a coat, and my wallet?" I asked the officer. It was the middle of March in Illinois. I had changed out of my work scrubs and was in the middle of my bedroom wearing a t-shirt, a pair of ISU sweatpants, and socks surrounded by the three officers. Nicole tried to retrieve the things I was requesting but one of the officers told her not to move.

The officer that handcuffed me bent down and whispered in my ear, "This is what happens to dykes. When you want to be a man, we treat you like a man. The only thing worse than a nigger is a nigger that's a dyke."

Tears raced down my face. I was alone, afraid, and devastated. I had never been in trouble and I had certainly never been in a police car. Nicole begged them not to take me to jail. She never wanted to file charges. She admitted to the officer that we both fought each other but they described me as the aggressor since I came home and initiated the confrontation.

I was led out of the apartment by the hateful officer who had handcuffed me. At this point I was terrified about what would happen when I was taken away from my home with no one to witness what would happen next. I was never allowed to obtain my shoes, keys, wallet or phone. The cold night air whooshed around me as I made my way to the squad car. My fingertips and toes getting frosty just in the short trip as I was pushed into the backseat. A small crowd had gathered outside to witness what had happened. I hung my head embarrassed and praying no one that I knew was there to see me at one of my lowest points.

What I experienced over the next two days in the county jail was deplorable. It was overcrowded and disgusting. There were no available cots, so I was forced to spend the two days laying on the cement floor with no pillow or blanket at night. The food looked like it was not even fit for a pig to eat so I had no water or food for the entire time I was there. I was forced to remove my braids and beads during the intake process so my hair was kinked and untamed. I was not able to shower so I felt disgusting. The small steel toilet in the corner of the cell was enough to make me vomit so I tried my hardest to not use the bathroom but could only hold out for so long.

At 9 o'clock PM each night, the lights automatically shut off and the holding cell housing the eight to ten women became pitch black. I prayed and asked God to cover me. I tried not to show fear or weakness, but it was apparent. I became a target and was picked on and attacked at least three times during my two days there. I was completely broken.

After the second day, two officers came to retrieve me from the place I literally thought I was going to die in. They placed my wrists in shackles and connected them to a chain that was fastened to another set of shackles that were secured around my ankles. I had to take quick tiny steps to try to keep up the pace the officers were making. I fought back tears as I wondered if this was the smallest glimpse as to what our ancestors went through. I was guided through various dimly lit hallways and passages. I had to struggle to climb stairwells until I finally surfaced into the public courtroom. Onlookers gazed at me as if I was the next murderer being brought before the judge. Several people leaned in and whispered while others just put their heads down so they did not have to make eye contact with me. I went before the judge who seemed to be annoyed by my very existence. After pleading my case explaining I was a college student, worked at the hospital, and had never been arrested before I was released to go home. I knew I owed this level of favor to God because I knew the officers and judge had it out for me.

I walked out of the front door of the county jail around 5 o'clock PM carrying nothing but what was left of my dignity and strength. Because I was denied the opportunity to obtain any of my belongings during my arrest, I was unable to catch a bus or taxi because I had no money. And to add insult to injury, Nicole was nowhere to be found and she would not have been able to pick me up anyway because she did not drive. I had no shoes on my feet. I was still in the same t-shirt, gray ISU sweatpants, and socks I was wearing when I was first introduced to this despicable place. Only now, they were stained with dirt, sweat, blood, and my tears from the days spent inside. I was forced to walk the twelve miles home wearing only the white socks that I had been wearing when all of this happened almost three days ago.

It took me almost four hours to get home. When I got about half of the way to my apartment, the sky opened and there was a downpouring of rain, which in hindsight I guess I was happy it was rain instead of snow since it was barely above freezing. I was wet, cold, weak, hungry, and thirsty. When I arrived home, there was a note on the door from Nicole. In the note she encouraged me to knock on the neighbor's door to obtain the apartment key. Luckily for me, the neighbor was home when I knocked.

"Hi. I'm sorry to bother you. My name is Candy and I live next door. Nicole said I would be able to get my key from you." I said softly.

The girl looked at me and you could tell she had a million questions and was probably a little afraid.

"Sure. Hold on." she said closing the door behind her.

I was able to get into the house within ten minutes. My white socks were soaked in water, brown and torn. There were small shards of glass stuck to my feet at the bottom. I limped over to the edge of the sofa in the living room and plopped down. I removed the socks and picked as much of the glass out as I could. All I wanted is to take a long hot bath and go to sleep. As I made my way to our bedroom, I instantly realized that all of Nicole's belongings were gone. There was no trace of her or the baby. She had left me. I tried to call her but it went straight to voicemail. I left message after message until I just gave up. As I bathed, I cried. My tears mixed with the water as they flowed and fell into the tub. I washed my hair multiple times as well as my body trying to rid myself of everything that had happened. I wanted to scrub away the scars, the stench of the jail, the feelings of the attacks…EVERYTHING. But the one thing that kept creeping back was the image of Nicole and Kendall I witnessed which set this entire thing in motion.

A week or so later I discovered that Nicole had moved in with Kendall. While they were beginning their relationship, I was forced to begin my journey. I had the daunting task of moving on, trying to rebuild, and heal physically and emotionally. She knew the role she played in the events that transpired at our home that night. She never filed charges, but the state picked up the case as they do in majority of the domestic calls they receive. This practice is done to minimize people calling the police in the heat of the moment and not really having any intention of filing charges. For the police, that is a waste of time and money.

I spent the next year or so fighting this case in court. How ironic. The college student majoring in Criminal Justice was being beat down by the same "justice system" she was learning about and was now beginning to feel like it was anything but just. I later graduated with my degree but could not do anything with it because of this blemish on my record. My dreams and goals had been shattered.

During this dark time, I was able to form a lifelong bond with my friend Wisdom. Wisdom would play an instrumental role during this time and many more in my life. This friend was the one that made me realize and accept that I could not just blame Nicole for me now having a record and having a degree that I could not utilize. I had to accept the actions and choices I made that night. I could have simply left when I felt myself losing control. But with all things in life, you must reap what you sow and accept the consequences that arise.

For years after this incident, I still had to deal with the decisions made that night. Sometimes the case would be seen when applying for jobs. I have had to submit formal letters explaining the details of what happened, my actions thereafter, and what has changed. I have felt as if I was having to explain why I am a decent human being and I deserve to be respected like the next person. I have even been denied apartments even though my credit was immaculate and I had a job. There have been some truly embarrassing and humiliating times all stemming from something that occurred over sixteen years ago. For a long time, it seemed as if I was unable to escape the critical mistake that I made at the age of twenty. My relationship with Nicole ended years ago but the effects of what we shared has stayed with me even today.

We were young and we moved extremely fast in our relationship but I loved Nicole freely and completely. I went into the relationship determined to hold nothing back and I wanted our love to be everything opposite of what I saw growing up. I wanted to love and be loved free of abuse, lies, and betrayal only to find all the things I was trying so desperately to avoid. I left my relationship with Nicole hurt beyond measure. I was disappointed that things turned out in the way they did but I spent several years waiting for anyone that followed to hurt or disappoint me in a similar manner. I became emotionally withdrawn and was unable and unwilling to love in the capacity that I once did.

The betrayal, abuse and abandonment that I felt after my relationship with Nicole would later become one of the heaviest suitcases that I ever had to unpack. I did not know how to express my feelings in a healthy manner. I lashed out when I was hurt. My grandma always said that hurt people hurt people and I made irrational emotional decisions that proved to be very costly to me in the long run. I hated who I became in my relationship with Nicole. I could not identify the person that I became. It took me years to be able to let go like I did with Nicole.

"In life you will be thrust into various situations in which you have no control. However, the one thing you do have complete control over is how you choose to respond."

- Candy

CHAPTER

Three

The Aftermath

My healing journey after Nicole was one of the hardest things I had to endure. The journey was long and came with its share of additional hurdles and setbacks. When you come out of a valley, you assume the light will be shining brighter and your life becomes better. This was not the case. My friend Wisdom told me that sometimes the end of one valley is just the start of another if the lesson you were supposed to learn you failed to do so. Or you could be catapulted into another valley if the character trait you are building still needs to be strengthened.

While in jail, I had missed two of my shifts at the hospital and was considered a "No Call, No Show". Due to the attendance policy at the hospital I lost my job. Luckily, I had one final check and I held on to that so I could have some resources while I looked for another job. To make matters worse, I returned home from class one day to find an envelope taped to the door from the leasing office. Inside was a notice to vacate and a copy of the portion of the lease with a section highlighted regarding disorderly conduct and noise violations. Due to my arrest I was asked to vacate the apartment within seven days.

I remember sitting on the couch, looking around the apartment at what remained, and I just started to cry. I was slowly losing everything. Where was I going to go with no job and no means to provide a deposit, rent, etc. I gathered my thoughts and realized at the end of the day, I was still a college student and the dorms were an option for students.

The next day I made my way to campus and entered the Office of Residential Life (ORL). I asked to speak to someone responsible for housing. The Spring semester was already in full swing so I was praying there would be an available room somewhere on campus. After the first few weeks of the semester started, there were always people who decided to leave because of transfers, they realize college is too much, or other reasons that you may never know. After explaining my situation, I felt like God was smiling down on me because there was a room available in Manchester Hall.

I was elated. I remember the lady asking me if I had financial aid and I gladly told her I had. That was how my tuition was covered. She advised me since I had only used it for tuition then I would still have the resources available for room and board. On top of that, I was also going to have a meal plan. Leaving out of ORL that day, it was the first day I felt like things were going to be ok. A sense of relief and calm came over me. I knew my 21st birthday was approaching and I was happy to know things were moving in a positive direction for my big day.

I moved into my little dorm room a few days later and settled into my routine of class and job hunting. One thing about living on campus is you do not need a lot of money due to your room and board being taken care of. Therefore, the little money I had managed to save I refused to touch except for necessities like toiletries. I knew I had to make sure I held on to as much money as I could until I found another job.

My 21st birthday came and went. I did not do much as I was happy to just have peace of mind which was a complete change from my 20th birthday. I had started hanging with my friend Jalisa again since Nicole and I had ended things. Jalisa never really cared for Nicole but tolerated her because she knew that was who I was in love with. We were having lunch one day in the dining center downstairs in my dorm.

"I am so happy to see a smile on your face." Jalisa said.

"I appreciate that. I still have my moments. I can honestly say I miss her but I know I'm better without her." I replied.

I was picking over my food and barely eating.

"What's wrong? You ok?" Jalisa quizzed.

"I'm good. I haven't had much of an appetite since everything happened."

Jalisa had no idea the extent I meant by that. Since Nicole and I had broken up I was barely eating, sleeping was hard, and I consumed myself with working out. My clothes were starting to fit loosely on me and I could see the weight leaving my face. Wisdom would joke with me and say, "you can tell how much you loved someone by how much weight you lose when you break up". I swear, everything she told me was indicative of what I was going through or something I realized later.

"I have noticed you lost some weight. You look good…sexy." Jalisa said flirtatiously.

I blushed. We always flirted back and forth but were the best of friends. We hung out a little longer talking and laughing and then she had to go. Before I headed upstairs to my room, I stopped by the bank of mailboxes so I could see if I had any mail. I pulled the couple of envelopes out and saw there was something from ORL and the financial aid office. I did not think anything of it and figured it was just confirmation of everything that had been done in the last few weeks.

I made my way up the elevator and into my room. I had already spent two hours working out earlier that morning so resting and watching television was the only thing on my mind right now. I laid across my bed and turned to BET. Thankfully, that was one of the good channels the university made available to us in the dorms. I was getting ready to drift off to sleep and I remembered the envelopes I had pulled from my mailbox.

I ripped open the first one from ORL and read over the letter. My stomach dropped. In the letter it stated I had no financial aid available for my room and board and I needed to contact the financial aid office immediately. What in the hell did they mean? How did I not have financial aid available when that was how my tuition was paid and I had not lived in the dorms at all this school year. I tore open the second letter from the financial aid office and the first thing that screamed at me from the pages was a balance of almost $5,000 that had to be paid within seven days or I had to provide proof of a private loan in the amount needed. This was needed for me to maintain my room and keep my meal plan.

I jumped up and immediately ran over to the phone in my room and made calls to ORL and the financial aid office. Over the next 30 minutes and speaking with several people I realized I was screwed. I learned yet another valuable and costly lesson as I sat there in my hard desk chair staring out the window at the campus below…financial aid refunds must come from somewhere. Those hefty refund checks I received at the beginning of each semester that was used for rent, bills, groceries, clothes, etc. had depleted the funds available for my room and board.

Where was I going to come up with almost $5,000 and within seven days on top of that? For the millionth time in the last couple of months, I cried. The mountain I thought I was climbing up had crumbled and fell on top of me. You would have thought that the best thing for me to do was to call back home and ask my family for the money. But that relationship was so strained because of me being gay and my relationship with Nicole that I did not dare. On top of that, my family had no idea of the events that had transpired since that horrible night in March. I knew calling on my family would have been me having to admit that everything I had fought against them for had failed and honestly, my pride would not allow them to have that satisfaction or be able to hold anything over my head.

Over the next couple of days, I continued to go to class because this was my senior year. I was so close to graduation. For me, it seemed like that was the only thing I could control and the one victory I would be able to walk away from all of this with. So in between my classes I would pray and try to research any potential options I could find. As the seven days wrapped up, I knew there was nothing I could do.

I had told Jalisa what was going on and she was there for me every step of the way. She helped me take all my belongings to a local storage facility down from the campus right off I-55. The only things I kept in my car with me were my clothes and toiletries. Jalisa said I could stay in her dorm with her. She was taking a huge risk for me because one of the major campus rules was no one should be living in your dorm room other than you or your roommate if you were assigned one. On top of that, she was a Resident Assistant (RA) who was responsible for all the young ladies on her floor to enforce the rules and be a resource. So, for her to be breaking one of the major dorm rules was huge.

"Are you sure about this?" I said as we returned to her dorm and were riding up the elevator.

"Candy, really? What do you think I was going to do? Let you sleep in the middle of the quad?" Jalisa said jokingly.

I felt terrible putting her in this situation. Not only was I dealing with my feelings of failure and inadequacy but I was now feeling guilty with what she was putting at stake. She could lose her position as an RA and even be put out of the dorms herself. In addition to that, Jalisa's girlfriend was not comfortable with me staying there. But I could not fault her for that. Honestly, I would not have felt comfortable with someone staying with my girlfriend in a small dorm room with only a twin sized bed. It also did not help that everyone thought we had dated. But we had not. We just had a close bond and playfully flirted but we never crossed the boundaries of a platonic friendship.

After about a week, I could not bring myself to stay with Jalisa any longer. My pride took over me and I could no longer ask her to sacrifice for me.

"Thank you for letting me stay here. I love you." I said to Jalisa as I was packing up my things.

"You're welcome. But you know I would do anything for you. I didn't know you had found a place though." Jalisa said.

"I haven't yet. But I have a friend off campus that is going to let me stay with her. Besides, I know you are tired of sleeping next to me and having my feet in your face." I joked.

The truth was, there was no friend and no off-campus apartment I was leaving to go to. I knew if I told Jalisa anything different, she would have never let me go. It was time for me to put my big girl panties on and truly sit in the aftermath of what all I had been through and done. My consequences were just that…mine.

The next several weeks were grueling. No one knew the degree of difficulty I was experiencing. At the end of the day, I was homeless and doing everything I could to continue going to class so I could graduate. I was signed up for 22 credit hours which equated to about seven classes. This was unheard of. I had obtained multiple overrides to even make this happen because the average course load was twelve to fifteen credit hours or four to five classes. So not only was I trying to prove a point because I wanted to prove it could be done but I knew I had to graduate this semester because I probably would not be able to come back another year.

I had lost my meal plan so I got very familiar with McDonald's dollar menu. The money I had left I had to make it stretch for as long as I could. I was so glad that I had a habit of hoarding money or else I do not know what I would have done for food, gas, toiletries, and trying to keep my cell phone on for as long as I could.

The one thing about being a college student is that it is easy to blend in. No one questioned when they saw me in the dining center warming up my cold McDonald's or Ramen noodles in one of the microwaves. I would see people in passing and always managed to say I was heading to class, a study session, work, or anywhere else I could think of to avoid lunch invitations I received from friends who would see me in random places around campus. Lunch dates usually consisted of everyone going to one of the dining centers and "swiping" our meals so we could sit and talk. But I knew I could not swipe my school ID because there were no funds available.

I had to do so much to maintain my hygiene and make sure I did not look like I had no place to lay my head at night. Thankfully, I had gotten my micro braids done for my birthday so despite them being a month or so old, I was still able to make them look presentable. I would carry my toothbrush, toothpaste, soap, and wash cloth in my messenger bag so I could wash up and brush my teeth in various bathrooms like the library, class buildings, and some of the dorms.

Every other day I would go out to Tri-Towers which was a set of the dorms that I did not know many people so I could shower. I would wait for the times when I knew a lot of people were gone to class in order to sneak up to one of the floors and into the bathroom to shower. I would inconspicuously pack everything in my messenger bag so in the off chance I ran into someone I would just appear as if I was passing through or visiting someone. I always showered as quick as I could and repacked everything back into my messenger bag. To leave, I would take the stairs instead of taking the elevator like I did when I came in. By taking the stairs, I could take a different door to leave. I never wanted the people at the front desk to catch on to my coming and going and prompt their suspicions to rise.

Every weekend I would make my way to a laundromat so I could wash my clothes, towels, and wash clothes in preparation for another week. There would be nights I would be parked in my car talking to God. I was seeking answers. As tears streamed down my face, I would be asking why this was happening to me. I needed the strength to keep going because I was so close to giving up. Was I insane not to take a little of the last money I had to put enough gas in my tank and make the hour and a half drive up I-55 North to Joliet? Was I being determined or stubborn? Strong or stupid? Accepting my consequences or causing myself undue stress? As I reclined the driver seat back as far as it would go and held my cell phone in my hand I stared up at the ceiling of the car. That was my scenery until I finally was able to drift to sleep and find the smallest sense of peace as I slept.

When finals week approached, I was so happy because that meant the library was now open 24 hours to allow students to study and finish any presentations or projects at any time they needed or wanted to. For me though, that meant a place I could sleep indoors rather than in my car. I would go up to the top floor where no one ever really went, find a corner in the back, pushed two chairs together, and gain some decent sleep. At least here in the library, I did not have to worry about finding a well-lit area to park my car and constantly jump every time I heard a noise outside of my car.

One day I was sitting in the computer lab concentrating on one of my projects I had to finish for one of my criminal justice classes. As I sat there typing away on the paper I was composing for class, I was approached by a young woman. She had dark curly hair, a light complexion, and was wearing a blue and white Zeta Phi Beta t-shirt.

"Excuse me. I'm sorry to bother you. My soror over there asked me to come and invite you to our party we have coming up." she said.

"Really?" I answered.

"Yeah. She's sitting over there."

I looked up and glanced across the computer lab and saw another lady wearing a similar blue and white t-shirt. She looked older and I assumed she was probably a graduate student. I waved being polite. She waved back and smiled.

"She didn't want to come and tell me herself?" I asked her young sidekick.

"No. She said she was busy but really wanted you to come out." she responded.

"Thank you for the invitation."

"You're welcome. See you around." she said as she retreated back across the computer lab.

This chance encounter in the library will prove to be the beginning of something huge later in my life and I had no idea. As I sat there thinking about the invitation I had just received, it was paradoxical how other students were living their lives carefree with only the stresses of finals. While, on the other hand, I was in a position where I was literally fighting to hold on.

I was broken. I was questioning almost everything about myself at that time. Thoughts of what my family used to tell me about being gay was a sin would infiltrate my mind in those moments when I was alone, hungry, and afraid. Was I being punished? Was I destined to fail because of what I felt naturally and for the person I was to my core? I was beginning to question so many aspects of my life and I was being tormented emotionally, spiritually, mentally, and physically.

Despite all the negative thoughts and feelings, I knew I had to press on. I knew I had to fight. I wanted to defy all the odds and prove all the naysayers wrong. There were times when Wisdom would tell me that it is at this moment when you feel like you cannot go on, when you feel like giving up, that is when you must push even harder because your breakthrough is near. She said that those who fail are the ones that get to that point and then run the other way. But those who get there and jump off the cliff, come out on the other side battered and bruised but victorious. I swear Wisdom always knows the perfect things to say at the perfect time.

One day I ran into Crystal. She was an old acquaintance a couple of my friends had introduced me to during the few weeks I stayed in the dorms earlier in the semester. She was a RA in the dorm I stayed in.

"Hey Candy. I haven't seen you in a while."

She was absolutely gorgeous. I remembered when I was introduced to her, I was smitten. She was tall, with a light complexion, and long beautiful hair. Her smile was infectious. But I learned she was not gay and honestly, I was still devastated by the loss of Nicole. Therefore, I just admired her from a far. But I never forgot about her because she was so positive and upbeat. Before having to leave the dorms, we had hung out and I really liked her spirit.

"Hey Crystal. Good to see you. I've just been busy with all these classes." I said.

She stopped and stared at me for a minute almost as if she was looking through my eyes into my soul.

"Just busy with classes?" she quizzed.

"Yeah. Remember I told you I'm taking 22 hours." I responded.

"I know. But that's not it." Crystal said.

I have no idea how she could tell there was something more to my story. No matter how much I tried to hide the truth, she knew it was more to it.

She grabbed my hand and said, "Let's go eat."

I panicked a little bit knowing that I had no meal plan, no extra money, and had to save face.

"I'm ok. I have to go finish studying."

Despite this, she insisted. I went with her to the dining center and we ate. She paid for my food and I opened up to her. She had no idea, as no one did, what I had been going through over the last few months. From that day, we spent more and more time together. And to my surprise, and the surprise of many others, we started dating. She allowed me to stay with her the way Jalisa had, which again, was against the university's dorm rules.

While staying with Crystal I finished the semester and graduated. I finally had a point on my side of the scoreboard. Despite this victory I still had a long way to go. Crystal and I dated for several months but unfortunately that relationship had to end for several reasons. I am grateful it was an amicable breakup and we are still friends to this day.

Life has a funny way of intertwining people into your life and crisscrossing paths. The older lady I met across from the computer lab was Chaun. I ended up running into her while I was dating Crystal and after I had graduated from ISU. Chaun and I had run into one another a couple more times around campus but the interactions never went past hello and exchanging names. Crystal and I had decided to go to one of the parties being held near campus which is something we never did. Chaun was there with her girlfriend as well.

"Hey Candy! How are you?" I heard coming from behind me and felt a slight tug on my arm.

"I'm good. How have you been? This is my girlfriend Crystal." I said pulling Crystal close to me.

Crystal and Chaun shook hands.

"This is my girlfriend Asia." Chaun reciprocated the introduction.

We stood in the line to enter the party engaging in conversation. Before the night ended Chaun and I exchanged numbers so we could all hang out again outside of the party setting. Crystal and I did not have any other couples we hung out with so we thought it would be cool. This was how the friendship started between Chaun and I and it began to flourish. As my relationship with Crystal ended and her relationship with Asia came to a dramatic end, we began to hang out together and truly get to know one another.

As I reflect on everything that happened it is interesting to know that someone that would become so instrumental in my life was present the whole time. Chaun did not learn any portion of this part of my life until we had been dating for months. I would share with her how one decision years ago caused a rippling domino effect in my life. It was reminiscent of taking a small pebble and throwing it into a pond and watching how the small rippling waves would expand outward from the center. That small pebble could disturb a leaf that was floating peacefully off in the distance. Even when Chaun and I started dating in 2006 I was just getting to a point where I could say the ripples had calmed from the splash made a few years prior.

"Every action that you make consciously or subconsciously influences your life. The aftermath could be small and insignificant or could be a tsunami that reshapes the entire foundation of your life. Choose wisely."

- Candy

CHAPTER

Four

Love Freely

After my relationship with Nicole I remained

guarded. I wanted love, stability and a long-term commitment but I was afraid of taking the risk of finding it. Every time I met someone, I remained an active part-time participant in the relationship having one foot in and one foot out just in case disappointment reared its ugly head.

I failed to learn how to completely let go of the hurt from past relationships until I accepted the fact that I was the force standing in the way of my very own happiness. I was my own worst enemy. I wanted one hundred percent from the person I attracted but expected them to be happy with the fifty percent of myself that I was willing to give. My actions hindered me until I fell in love with the person that made me want to be a better woman.

I had no idea that the woman I met in Milner Library while I was homeless and struggling to make it would end up becoming so much more to me. When Chaun and I started our friendship, I had no intentions on pursuing a relationship with her. I looked at her as someone to talk to and pass the time with. I was pleasantly surprised to learn there was so much more to her. Once we decided to take things beyond just the friendship realm we moved at a rapid pace. It was easy for us to do so since we had formed a friendship and created a bond. We were able to talk to one another about anything and that was refreshing for me. I had spent so much time keeping things to myself, hiding the truth, and putting up a façade. With Chaun, I did not have to do that. I could be me and be completely free.

About five months into our relationship it was time for me to renew my lease to my apartment in College Station. I had been living with my roommate for a year. However, Chaun was living in Peoria and I was living in Bloomington. Even though it was only 45 minutes away, I wanted to be closer to her. I wanted to be able to see her every day. That for me, was a sign that the wall I had built around my heart was weakening and beginning to crumble. I still was guarded but I could feel the shift.

Our relationship continued to grow. Our bond as friends was strong but our chemistry as lovers was unmatched. We were young and in love. The world was our playground and we maximized every chance we had to improve ourselves and build a solid future together.

We truly took the time to bond and have fun with one another. On sunny Sunday afternoons we would go get ice cream from Cold Stone or Dairy Queen then take long drives through the affluent neighborhoods that housed the palatial estates that we dreamed of. As I drove, Chaun picked out the staircase and layout of each level. She described the rooms of our imaginary kids and I described the cars that I wanted in our circular brick paved driveway. We wanted the same things: stability, loyalty and companionship. We promised to not just be lovers but partners.

As we drove through those neighborhoods, we would remember the addresses with the "For Sale" signs posted in the yard so we could research the price of the homes and take our own virtual open house tours. We hoped to one day own and no longer rent. We took immediate action to improve our credit because we hoped to purchase our first home within five years or so. Four years later we were closing on our first home. It was a three bedroom, two and a half bath, two story home.

We had been in our careers for a couple of years within the same company and we were both on the track for management. A few months after closing on our home, Chaun and I enrolled in a master's Program in pursuit of our MBAs. Looking back, it is evident that this was one of the happiest times of my life. I was committed to a woman that made me want to be a better person. She loved me. She challenged me. She supported me. She made me happy. And in return, I wanted to give her all that she gave to me and a little more.

There was something about this woman that made me want to believe in love again. Even though we were business minded and did things each day as steps to our ultimate plan, we never stopped enjoying each other. We had so much fun with each other. She was truly my best friend as well as my partner. We did everything together and I would not have wanted it any other way. There were many reasons why I knew Chaun was special and different from any other woman I had dated but it was on a trip to Minnesota that it truly sunk in.

"Have you ever been to the Mall of America?" I asked Chaun.

"No. Is it nice?"

"It's huge. I went years ago when I was in the gospel choir in high school. There are tons of things to do. We should go." I said with excitement in my voice. I loved exposing Chaun to new things. I loved to see the look in her eyes and live through those moments with her.

"Sounds fun to me. When do you want to go?" she asked.

"Whenever you want to. We can make a weekend of it."

We looked at the calendar and chose a weekend. The next day we both requested the days off work we needed so we could make the almost seven-hour drive and still have time to enjoy the trip. After getting our requests approved, we booked our hotel room and were ready for our adventure. This was the first major trip we had taken together.

During this trip we got lost in one another. During the drive we listened to music, joked, and laughed. I found myself at times looking over at her and realizing that no matter what I did I always wanted her by my side. Throughout the weekend we walked through the mall, took in multiple attractions, and enjoyed our quality time with each other. When we would make our way back to the hotel after a full day of activities, we would lay in one another's arms reliving the fun times we had encountered during the day. Nothing else mattered for me. I knew I was falling deeper and deeper in love with Chaun. The fact that I could not imagine myself doing this or anything else with anyone but her made me realize I was stepping into unchartered territory with my emotions.

She made me feel safe and I knew it was acceptable for me to give as much of me as I wanted of her. I had heard a quote before about love that I loosely adopted because I truly connected to the words. I believe that love is giving someone the ability to destroy you but trusting they will not. Inserting the word "destroy" was more my doing after experiencing what I did with Nicole. I knew I was in love with Chaun. The only question that remained was, why not marry her? We had been together for four years and I saw myself with her forever. That trip to Minnesota solidified so many things for me. I knew I was ready to take the ultimate step with Chaun. I just had to decide when and how I was going to do it.

I decided to plan a romantic weekend in Chicago for Chaun and I. I envisioned us making the two hour drive up for the weekend spending time in a fancy hotel and enjoying some of the best downtown amenities the city had to offer. I had grown tired of the traditional dinner and movie sort of weekend we had grown accustom to and I was ready to expand our horizons.

But I had made up in my mind that I wanted this woman to be my wife. I wanted to make this seemingly simple weekend something she would never forget. I was ready to propose. The plans to make everything perfect took me a few months to execute. Keeping this a surprise was going to be the major test, not only for Chaun but also for me. I personally do not like surprises and it is usually hard for me to keep a surprise for someone else as well.

"I am looking forward to this weekend." Chaun said one day as we were sitting in our TV room watching TV.

"Me too. It will be good to get from down here and do something different for a change."

"So, you still not going to tell me where we're going?" she quizzed.

She knew normally if she pressed, I would break and tell her all the details she wanted to know. But this time I was strong and did not falter. I had to pull this off.

"No. But just make sure you pack something nice to wear in case we find a nice restaurant or something."

"Ok."

The weekend was finally here and it was time for me to do one of the biggest things I had ever done before in my life. We took our bags and tossed them in the trunk of my black Maxima and headed towards Chicago. Once Chaun and I arrived in Chicago, our first stop was to her mother's house. As we approached the tall southside apartment building I leaned over and kissed Chaun's cheek.

"Listen closely babe. I need you to grab your bag and be dressed by four." I smirked.

"Where are you going baby?" she asked.

I grabbed her chin and pulled her close, "Don't ask me no questions about where I'm going or what I'm doing because I have a surprise for you. Just go in, spend time with your mom and be ready at four."

"Oooh…look at you putting your foot down. Ok. I love you. I'll be ready." she said as she kissed me and got out of the car.

I sat and watched until she made it safely into the building. It was now go time. I looked at the time on my dashboard and it was a little after 12:30. My heart started to race and the nerves were now kicking in. But I had no time. I had things to do and only three hours to get it all done.

By 4:00 PM a long black stretch limousine approached the southside apartment building I had left Chaun at just a few hours earlier. As the limo driver exited to open my door a small crowd of onlookers from the neighborhood had started to form. Everyone was looking to see why the limo was there. The driver had arrived at the rear door and opened it. He expertly reached out to grab my hand to assist me as I exited the limo.

"We've arrived ma'am," he announced.

"Thank you very much," I replied.

I reached back into the limo to grab the first surprise I had for Chaun that was carefully wrapped in the back seat with me. The nervousness began to set in again as I stood still in my tailor cut black Tahari pants suit. I took a deep breath and made my way to the door of the building. Chaun's sister's and mom had somehow saw me and knew I was on my way to the building so they had already started buzzing me in.

I entered the gray stone building and took a deep breath as I opened the second door leading to the stairs. It seemed like it took me an hour to go up the one flight of stairs. I knocked to signal I had made it in and was at the door. Chaun opened the door and was beaming. The smile on her face could have lit up downtown Chicago.

"Hi baby! Those are beautiful. Oh my goodness!" she squealed reacting to the bouquet of flowers I was holding in my arms. What she did not know is I had arranged to go to a florist that was willing to let me come and create the bouquet myself. I wanted it to be unique and something that was only for her which included her favorite flower along with other of the more traditional flowers.

"Hey babe." I handed her the bouquet and hugged and kissed her.

"Are you ready to go?"

"I am! Mom I'll see you guys later. Love you!" Chaun said as she hugged and kissed her mom.

Chaun's mom looked at me and winked. In the weeks leading up to this weekend I had already talked to Chaun's mom, grandmother, and great-grandmother to gain their blessing prior to proposing. Each of them gave me their blessing without hesitation. So, they knew it was coming but they had no idea what I had planned.

We made our way back outside and the driver was waiting outside the limo for us. He opened the door and assisted us into the vehicle. As we pulled away from the building, I pushed play on the radio controls I had access to in the rear of the limo. A list of songs began to play from a CD I had created earlier in the week specifically for this moment. I had cleverly titled it "The Question". On there were songs from artists like Luther Vandross, Kelly Price, and Maxwell. As the music played, I looked over at Chaun and she was looking at me smiling and I noticed a couple of tears streaming down her face.

"What's wrong?"

"No one has ever done anything like this for me before. I just love you so much and am just enjoying the moment." She replied.

Wiping the tears from her cheeks I kissed the back of her hand I was holding, "I love you and I just want you to know how much."

"He Proposed" by Kelly Price was playing as we made our way down the Dan Ryan expressway toward downtown Chicago. Her sultry voice singing:

"My baby took me to a special place

Said he had a surprise for me

He told me to close my eyes

So that I could not see and when I opened them up

He was on one knee reachin' for my hand

That's when he proposed to me...."

The butterflies in my stomach began to flutter again. The limo pulled in front of the tall 92 story glass skyscraper illuminated with golden lights.

"Do you know where we are?" I asked Chaun.

She peered out the window and saw the large letters lit up part way up the side of the building.

"Trump Towers!" She exclaimed.

The doorman for the hotel came to the curbside door and opened it to allow Chaun and I to exit the car.

"Good evening Ms. Johnson. Welcome back." the doorman said as I exited the limo. I was hoping Chaun did not catch on to what he said considering she had no idea I had been here earlier in the day.

"Thank you." I replied.

I held Chaun's hand as we entered the lobby through the glass revolving doors.

"Good evening Ms. Johnson." the receptionist stated as she saw me walking toward the bank of elevators.

"Good evening." I said. Again, I hoped Chaun had not noticed the receptionist had addressed me by name. But she was too busy looking around and admiring the two-story lobby with its glass windows, shiny marble floors, and other plush elegant décor.

We entered the elevator and I selected our floor discreetly using the room key so she would not be aware.

"I have to show you something before we continue on with our night." I said.

"Ok." Chaun said looking a little puzzled but respecting what I said earlier about not asking any questions.

We exited the elevator and I had her take a seat in the small purple plush chair that was eloquently situated across from the elevators.

"Wait here. I'll be right back."

I went to the room to make sure everything was in place how I needed it to be. My hands were sweating and I knew this was the moment I had been anticipating. I was preparing to ask the question that would change my life. I went back to Chaun and grabbed her hand. We walked down the hallway and I lead her to our suite.

"Are you ready?" I asked.

"Yes." she said sweetly.

I pushed the door open and Chaun was greeted by a saxophone player and keyboardist dressed neatly in black suits, polished black loafers, white button up shirts and black bow ties. Rose petals lined the floor leading the path to where they were standing in front of the glowing fireplace. The drapes were pulled back to expose the view of the neighboring downtown Chicago skyscrapers and Lake Michigan. As Brian McKnight's "Back at One" was being expertly played I lead Chaun to the couch in front of the musicians.

When we took our seats, I held Chaun's hands and I noticed a couple of tears running down her face again.

"You ok?" I asked.

"This is beautiful." she said to me.

"I have something I need to ask you before we continue on with our night." I said nervously.

Chaun looked at me as if she was hanging on to my every word. I wondered then if she had finally figured it all out. Had she caught on to the subtle clues that had been before her the entire evening.

"Yes." she said.

I reached behind the pillow that was next to me and pulled out the ring box. I got down on one knee between the couch and the coffee table. I grabbed her left hand and looked deep into her eyes, "I want to know if you would do me the honors of being my wife and spend the rest of your life with me."

A huge smile spread across Chaun's face and the tears began to fall again. "Yes!" she exclaimed as she wrapped her arms around me.

"You knew about this!" she shrieked at the musicians. They remained professional and continued to belt out more melodic love songs.

I let out a joyful laugh and placed the ring on her finger. I was the happiest woman in the world right then. I sat back holding Chaun's hand reflecting on how far I had come while we listened to the musicians play. I had finally been able to love freely again which was something I had not done in years. My guard was completely down and I knew that it was possible to love again. I knew that even though your heart can endure the highest levels of hurt and devastation, it can recover and it was acceptable to be vulnerable and it felt amazing.

We continued and had dinner at the Signature Room in the John Hancock Building. That night nothing or no one else mattered. It was just her, me, and our love and that was all I needed. This was the beginning of the rest of our lives together.

"You will never truly be healed if you refuse to jump the same hurdle you fell over, drive down the same path you got lost, or climb the same mountain you fell down. True healing comes in overtaking what once overtook you."

- Candy

CHAPTER

five

Married Twice

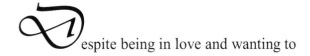espite being in love and wanting to spend the rest of our lives together, it was not as easy as it seemed. We had so many people standing behind us and sharing in our joy. Unfortunately, at the time we wanted to get married, it had not become legal in the state of Illinois yet. The legalization of gay marriage in other states had caused tons of couples to flock to local courthouses and wedding venues to profess their love in the hopes of securing the same rights as our heterosexual counterparts. Because of this, we made the decision to get married… twice.

We researched to find the states where gay marriage was legal. The closest state for us was Iowa. Neither of us had ever been to Iowa. But what better reason to visit for the first time than to dedicate our lives to one another. Chaun found an officiate in Iowa City that would marry us and determined the necessary steps and forms needed to solidify our union.

We took the drive to Iowa City over the flat lands and cornfields. We listened to music, talked, and laughed as we always did. I was extremely happy to be taking this step in my life but sad all at the same time. I met and fell madly in love with the woman I planned on spending the rest of my life with. However, I was sad that we had to drive across states in order to do it. We had to take additional steps, take extra time off work, and travel to complete a step that others could easily do at any time.

At the time, we were not given the same rights as everyone else. While we were on our way to make memories, the country was in turmoil over same sex marriage and so was my family. This trip meant the world to us but the world knew nothing about it. For our friends and some family members it was just Chaun and I spending time with each other for my birthday. I had no true family support. Nobody knew what we were doing.

My level of emotion was high as I processed my thoughts and emotions about everything that was going on in this single act of love. I was happy in my relationship and my future marriage but I was also very afraid. In that moment, the woman sitting in the passenger seat with me was my everything. I felt like it was all or nothing and Chaun was all I had. But despite it all, I was fine with that. I would not have chosen it to be any other way. She made me feel comfortable during the pain and rejection I felt from my family. Every time I felt alone, she would be there for me to comfort me and support me so that I felt like she was all I needed.

We did not just promise in sickness and in health or for better and for worse, we promised to the end of time. We made plans to conquer the world together. We always swore that it was her and I against anything and everyone. We did so privately so there would be no room for distractions or interruptions in what I felt was God's plan.

We arrived in Iowa City and checked into Hotel Vetro. It was a modern and elegantly designed hotel in downtown Iowa City. It was in a perfect location close to the University of Iowa and surrounded by stores, cafes, pubs, and more. The weather was great for late March and we walked around downtown Iowa City taking the sights. We lucked up and found a good place to eat.

"Are you ready for tomorrow?" Chaun asked as we ate.

"Absolutely." I said.

"I can't believe we are doing this." she said through a smile.

"Well believe it. You are about to be my wife."

The next day we got up and got dressed so we could meet the officiate and the witnesses at the county courthouse. We took the short drive and arrived at the building that was reminiscent of a small medieval castle. It had perfectly manicured grass and bushes welcoming those that were coming and going. The process took about an hour to complete but when it was all said done, we walked out of the courthouse married and legally attached to one another now in addition to being emotionally and spiritually attached.

As we left the courthouse, we stopped under one of the trees in front. The officiate took several pictures for us so we could memorialize that moment that no one knew about. I was the happiest I had been in a long time and I could tell by the smile on Chaun's face that she felt the same way. We spent the rest of the afternoon exploring more of downtown before deciding to go back to our room and spend time with just each other.

We stopped at the store that was connected to the hotel to grab snacks and rented a couple of movies since there was a DVD player provided in the room. We made our way back to the contemporary styled room with the floor to ceiling windows. The lights from downtown were twinkling in the background. Chaun and I showered so we could get comfortable and settle in for the night. In addition to the king bed, there was a tan chaise lounge that I had grown to like as well. It was shaped like a wave and allowed you to settle in like you were resting in the palm of someone's hand.

I had settled in the chaise and Chaun had laid across the king bed after putting in one of the movies we had rented. I had on my black basketball shorts and a t-shirt trying to pay attention to the movie that was playing. I was never much of a movie person but Chaun was so I always made time to enjoy them with her. About fifteen minutes into the movie, Chaun slid off the bed and came over to me.

"Hey wifey." she said as she leaned down and kissed me.

"Hey boo."

She took her long beautiful caramel legs and draped them across me and the chaise and sat in my lap. It was then I noticed she only had on a t-shirt and panties. She leaned down and started placing sweet tender kisses on my cheek and down my neck. I wrapped my arms around her and pulled her closer.

"I love you." she whispered in my ear.

"I love you more." I responded as I took in the sweet smell of the Japanese Cherry Blossom lotion she was wearing.

As she continued to plant kisses on both sides of my neck, I knew we were not going to finish watching the movie that was playing softly in the background. I removed her t-shirt and exposed her plump full breasts. I took my hands and caressed her back as she leaned in closer to allow me to suckle on her nipples like she knew I liked to do. As I sucked on her nipples, I could hear her softly begin to moan. Her head fell back and she began to grind on my lap softly.

She reached down and removed my shirt. She leaned down and kissed me again allowing her skin to touch mine. Her kisses made a trail from my lips down my neck and to my nipples and my wetness began.

I ran my hands through her hair as she woke my body up like only she knew how. She stood up and placed her hands under my waist guiding me to lift my bottom up just enough for her to be able to slip my basketball shorts down. It was something so sensual about this moment that seemed different than the times before. Chaun seemed to be looking at me like I was a completely different person. We locked eyes for a moment and it was like a transference of souls.

She had me scoot down a little in the chaise lounge so that my pelvis was elevated and guided my legs apart so that my feet were on the ground. She got down on her knees in front of me and started kissing and licking on my legs. She started at my calves and made her way up past my knees and then between my thighs. She took her tongue and teased me by going closer to my center and then going back down my thighs a bit. She knew what she was doing. My body was begging her to dive in. I placed my hand on her head trying to beckon her to me.

She finally gave in and started to feast on my sweetness. She slowly licked and sucked on my center bringing me closer and closer to climax. I held her head so she was sucking on my clit. I wanted to hit my peak.

"No baby. Not yet." she said.

She slowed her pace and decreased the intensity so I would not cross the finish line yet. She massaged my breasts with her hands as she slowly indulged in my juices. I felt her pause for a moment but I was so lost in the pleasure that I had no idea she had grabbed a vibrator that she must have strategically placed out of sight. The low humming filled the room and intertwined with the sound of the movie playing in the background.

Suddenly I felt the vibration on the inside of my thighs and my body quivered. She teased my thighs with the vibrator as she went back to tasting me. She licked and sucked me so passionately that I started to feel a wave of warmth go through my body. I was so close to exploding and she knew it because my body began to stiffen. Before I could climax the soft wet feeling from her tongue was replaced by the vibration I had been feeling on my thighs. The end was growing near and before I knew it, I had exploded in the chair.

My orgasm took over me and I enjoyed every moment of it. While I was riding my orgasmic wave, she entered me and I exploded all over again. She made love to me like the rest of the world did not matter. She was so in tune with my body and had my body doing things it had never done before. She pleased me until I had to beg her to stop so I could express my love and desire for her.

We made our way to the bed and I removed her panties. I explored every inch of her body with my lips and my tongue. I wanted to express my undying love for her. This woman was now my wife and the passion and the love we had for one another was evident as we made love over and over that night. My level of happiness was insurmountable that night and I felt safe, loved, and secure in the decision that I had made to spend the rest of my life with Chaun.

After our three days in Iowa City we returned to our world and the plans for the public wedding continued. Despite already being married, we still wanted to have the wedding ceremony for our family and friends. We had already made the commitment but we also wanted to make the commitment in front of those that we love and that loved us. We chose July 16th as our wedding day for no specific reason other than hoping to have good weather and liking the idea of having a summer wedding. It was going to be the culmination of the previous five years of our relationship. It was the day Chaun was going to become my wife…again. Chaun spent months planning and preparing for this day. She had even convinced me to wear a wedding dress…go figure!

Even though it was going to be a joyous occasion, making the decision to live in your truth often forces others to live in theirs. What was supposed to be one of the most important days of my life was the source of contention within my immediate family that caused people to take sides. My mom was not in support of me marrying a woman but she loved her child. Her love for me came first and took precedence over her lack of acceptance of who I fell in love with. Not only had she agreed to attend the wedding but she was also willing to be an active participant in the ceremony.

Other than my mom, there was a clear divide between the rest of my immediate family. My grandparents and my aunt were completely against me being with a woman. Because of their feelings and their religious stance on it they made the decision to not attend the wedding. This hurt me to my core because they meant the world to me. To know the closest people to me were not going to be present to support me was devastating. I did have a host of cousins, aunts, uncles, and friends that did attend and show me support no matter what. Their love allowed them to be there for me whether they agreed with me loving a woman or not.

Chaun knew the turmoil I was going through and the pain I felt amid my happiness. She was nothing but supportive through everything.

"What's wrong?" Chaun asked one day while we were talking about the wedding.

"I think I want to write letters to my family so they can know how I feel and how important the wedding is for me." I responded.

"Are you sure you want to do that? I am not saying you shouldn't but you have to be prepared for whatever the outcome may be."

Chaun was speaking from experience because she had done the same with her family years ago for other reasons. They were all received well except for one and she just wanted to make sure I knew the risk that was involved.

"I know what you mean. But I think it is something I have to do. I want everyone to know how I really feel and writing the letters will allow me to be able to fully express myself uninterrupted."

"That is true. I am praying it goes well and you get the outcome that you want and deserve." Chaun said.

After bearing my soul and being completely transparent with my family in the letters I said a prayer over them and put them in the mail. At that point it was out of my hands and I had to allow the chips to fall as they may. Unfortunately, even after the letters my grandparent's and aunt's stances remained the same.

The months passed and the wedding weekend was quickly approaching. Yet again, I had the feeling of being happy but sad at the same time. I had to go into the weekend knowing that my wife's family was there in full support on both sides of her family but I only had a small representation from one side of my family. The feelings of rejection and abandonment were intertwined in my excitement and love that I had for Chaun. Yet in still, I put a smile on my face and put my best foot forward for her.

"Babe, are you sure you liked the favor bags?" Chaun asked excitedly as she packed the hundred plus bags in the plastic bin so we could transport them to the hotel where the wedding would be held that weekend.

"Yes babe. You did a great job on them." I replied as I focused on my laptop going through emails to make sure I had not missed anything before I leave for our wedding weekend.

"I am so excited!" Chaun squealed.

I smiled as I watched her race around the house making sure our wedding dresses were packed, our toiletries were in our suitcase, our shoes, rings, and the bouquets she had made were all accounted for. This was a big deal and you could tell she wanted to make sure everything was perfect.

"Where did you put the programs?" she asked

"The what?"

"The programs for the reception. Are they still in the office from when we printed them?"

"No. I put them in the bin with the wishing well, cake topper and the other stuff." I responded.

Everything was packed and we were ready to take the trip the next day to Rosemont where we would be staying for the weekend. We had chosen the Crowne Plaza Hotel after visiting numerous options. We had no idea the notoriety it would later have in September 2017. But on July 16th, 2011 it was the setting for us to profess our love and commitment to one another in front of our family and friends.

The day came and for Chaun and I we were consumed with nerves and excitement. Everything appeared to be perfect. The ceremony room looked amazing. There was a white altar at the front of the room accompanied by a high table with an elegantly laced white tablecloth. Placed on the table were two heart shaped glass jars that represented Chaun and I. One was filled with brown sand and the other with celadon colored sand, which was our wedding colors. Later in the ceremony we would pour our sands into a third glass jar that would signify the uniting of our lives forever.

The reception area was awesome as well. The tall ceiling housed an ornately decorated chandelier comprised of beautiful lights and ivory colored chiffon material. The banquet tables were expertly decorated with white tablecloths, brown table runners, and glass fishbowl centerpieces with celadon colored pebbles in each. The tealight candles glowed softly from each table. We stood there mesmerized for a moment but knew we had to get going. We raced to get ready because we were adamant that we did not want to fall prey to the typical late wedding start time. We held to that as closely as we could and the wedding started within fifteen minutes of its scheduled start time.

As promised, my mother was there and participated in the ceremony. My younger brother supported me and walked me down the aisle.

As I stood nervously at the alter waiting for Chaun to enter I was filled with happiness knowing that I was dedicating my life to her for a second time for everyone to witness. When the large mahogany wood doors opened and she appeared in her white gown I was taken aback by her beauty. She was absolutely stunning. She stood tall with her micro braids styled graciously into an updo with a tiara perfectly placed as the additional tendrils cascaded to frame her face. Her makeup was expertly done and enhanced the almond shape of her eyes and her gorgeous high cheekbones. She graciously walked down the white runner that was lined with rose petals as our family and friends looked on snapping pictures and some shedding tears. Everything about that moment was perfect.

We stood there holding hands and exchanged our vows. We promised to cherish one another and to always be a support to each other. We also promised that despite becoming one, we would never lose sight of our individuality and embrace one another's differences. We would stand together against any and all adversity as a unified front and not allow anything or anyone to come between us. As we made those promises to one another as everyone looked on, I was confident that we both meant every word we said to one another.

The ceremony ended and we took pictures while our guests enjoyed the cocktail hour. We entered the reception and the rest of the night flew by. Before we knew it, the night was ending and we retired to our room. We reflected on the day's events and finally had time to rest. As we were able to wash away the makeup, remove the wedding gowns, and relax, my mind drifted to the still sore spot that I had in my heart. I went back to thinking about the guests and most importantly, the ones that chose not to be guests.

I knew my family loved me and I was certain of this but it hurt me to know that I caused so much heartache, disappointment, and division. I had done all this even though I felt like all I was doing was choosing love and my happiness. Whether I knew it or not, people felt obligated to take a side or defend their principles. So, during my happiness, I was left with a level of guilt and remorse because of those that chose not to come.

As I lay there in the plush king-sized bed of our suite, I held my wife tightly in my arms. As she softly slept on my chest, I stared at her for what seemed like hours and I felt afraid. I knew this woman I had chosen is where I had laid all my trust and as I lay there reflecting, tears slowly slid down my face. And to this day, I am not sure if I should classify those as tears of joy, tears of pain, or a combination of the two.

"Making the decision to live your truth often forces others to also live in theirs…whether they choose to or not."

- Candy

CHAPTER
Six

Never Lose Sight on What's Important

We never had a honeymoon like most couples have so they can sit back and enjoy the idea that they made the ultimate commitment to one another. We literally were married on Saturday and were back to work on Monday. Even though we did not have the traditional honeymoon in Jamaica, Mexico, or some other exotic or extravagant place, we spent the first few months after the wedding making one another our own personal honeymoons.

Chaun and I spent time with one another planning our future. We knew this was not the end for us and everything we did from that moment forward was a step to reach that goal. We could barely stand to be away from one another when we did not have to. We worked together, took our breaks together, and just enjoyed being with each other. We would laugh when our family, friends, and coworkers would joke about how they could never be around their spouse or significant other the way we were.

I think for some it was a little sickening and for others they may not have believed what they witnessed was the truth. But it absolutely was. We decided we were ready to expand our little family. I went out and got a golden Pomeranian Poodle that Chaun fell in love with instantly when she saw her.

"Oh my goodness! She is adorable!" Chaun squealed.

"Do you like her?" I asked a little nervous considering I made this huge purchase without talking to Chaun first.

We had been talking about getting a dog for a little while. Chaun was always a cat lover but I absolutely could not entertain the thought of having a cat in the house. So, we compromised on a dog. We knew we wanted a small dog and had looked at various breeds like Yorkies, Terriers, and even some teacup breeds. But when I went to the pet store, I immediately saw this little Pomeranian Poodle and knew she was the perfect one.

"I love her! What's her name?" Chaun asked.

"I don't know. That's going to be up to you. They called her Sadie at the pet store but I was pretty sure that was not going to stick" I chuckled.

Sadie got comfortable with us right away. She strutted around the house as if she had lived there for years.

"She walks like she's switching. She's a little diva." Chaun laughed. "That's it! Diva!"

"Works for me." I laughed

I could not have asked for anything more. My life was close to perfect and I had my wife right by my side. As time progressed, Chaun and I decided it was time for us to start taking the additional steps towards achieving more of the goals we had for ourselves and our future. We both decided we wanted to return to school to obtain our master's degrees in Business Administration. Since we were both on the management track with our company, we were advised by our mentors that having our MBA along with additional industry certifications would strengthen our portfolios when being considered for advancement. We had both started working on our graduate degrees a couple of years prior so when we returned, we only had about a year left to complete the program.

While taking courses to complete our graduate program I had also made the decision I was ready to join our beloved sorority, Zeta Phi Beta Sorority, Inc. Chaun was already active in the chapter and juggling those responsibilities, working full time, and taking graduate classes. After joining I had to add those additional tasks to my plate.

If that was not enough, I was approached at work with an amazing business opportunity I had not thought about. I was informed about another career path I could take with the company where I could own my own business and be a business owner. This spoke to my heart as I had always had an entrepreneurial spirit. I had tried my hands at a few things before but nothing to this magnitude.

I remember driving home excited to tell Chaun about the opportunity. I parked my black Nissan Maxima in the garage next to Chaun's royal blue Mitsubishi and raced in the house. I came in and the first floor was dark which meant Chaun was upstairs. She was probably working on schoolwork as we typically did when we came home from work. I grabbed me a bottle of water out of the refrigerator. Part way to the stairs I stopped and turned back around to go back to the refrigerator. I grabbed a second bottle of water for Chaun so I could make sure she had something to drink as well.

I climbed the stairs and I could see the light coming from our office. I walked in quietly as Chaun was sitting at the desk with her face buried in the computer screen. I set the bottle of water I brought for her on the desk next to her and leaned down and kissed her on the cheek.

"Hey baby. I missed you." She said as she reached back to grab me.

"I missed you too. Babe, I need to talk to you." I said.

"What's up?" she stopped and turned around in the chair to give me her undivided attention.

"Can we go in the room so I can get out these clothes and get comfortable." I asked.

"Why don't you go shower and get comfortable so that will give me enough time to finish these couple of posts for class."

"Ok. I'll see you in the room." I turned to head towards the door.

"And thank you for the water babe. How did you know I was thirsty?" Chaun asked.

"Don't I always know when you are thirsty, or want a snack, or whatever."

She smiled and looked at me while I walked out the office to head to our bedroom. About thirty minutes later I had finished showering and getting changed. Chaun had finished her schoolwork and we decided to go downstairs to the TV room so I could tell her all about the opportunity I had learned about today.

"What did you want to talk to me about?" Chaun asked as we turned the TV on to find something to watch.

"So, my manager came to me today and was telling me about this opportunity I can take and I am pretty interested in it."

"Well what is it?" she quizzed.

"Well, I could leave the corporate side of the business and become an agent and have my own office." I said excitedly.

"Really?" she asked inquisitively.

I knew her wheels were already turning because Chaun was not the risk taker between the two of us. I am sure what I just said translated into a huge risk and losing the guaranteed income we had grown accustomed to. We had shaped our lives around our salaries, built our credit, purchased our first house, and was saving money. I could tell by her eyes she was a little nervous but she is one of the most supportive people I know. She listened as I explained everything the way it was explained to me.

"When is the informational meeting they want you to attend?" she asked.

"Next week. Are you ok with me looking further into it?" I asked nervously.

"Of course. If that is what you want to do then you need to learn as much as you can so you can decide if it is the best thing for you."

"Are you sure you're ok with it?" I probed. I knew Chaun was slow in expressing her true feelings and did not like to communicate. I would hate to find out later down the line she really was not in support of me exploring this. There was a pregnant pause between us before she responded.

"Yes. I'm ok with it."

I trusted she meant what she said and forged ahead with my plan in exploring this opportunity. I attended the informational meeting the following week and I was even more intrigued. I decided to take the plunge and redirect my career path. While pursuing this agent opportunity I was subjected to numerous interviews and multiple steps before I could officially be chosen. During the interview process I had to continue my current role on the corporate side all while keeping up with my prior commitments with school and my sorority.

There was a lot going on all at once. Amid everything I had noticed a shift in the dynamic with Chaun and I. We seemed to be growing distant and the unbreakable connection I once felt with her seemed like it was deteriorating. But I refused to allow past hurts to sabotage the incredible relationship I had with my wife. Besides, we had a lot of demands on our plates and I attributed the distance to the stress we were both under.

The last interview I had to become an agent I was urged by leadership to bring Chaun with me because this was going to be a life altering decision. They explained how they liked for candidate's partners and spouses to have the opportunity to be present and ask questions to ensure the decision was being made with all parties on board.

"I am nervous and I am not even the one going for the opportunity." Chaun said as we made the drive north toward Chicago.

I giggled a little bit trying to control my own nerves. "Don't be nervous baby. But remember you can ask any questions you want to ask so you fully understand."

"Ok. I will." she said.

We pressed through the interview that lasted for a couple of hours. When it was all said and done, I was blessed with the opportunity. From that moment forward, we both had tunnel vision. I was focused on opening the business, completing my coursework to graduate, and now having to uproot and relocate. Chaun had her graduation and finding a new position in our new location.

Through it all, Chaun was supportive but the connection we shared continued to diminish. Our intimacy was fading and we were becoming more and more like ships passing in the night. It seemed like our life shifted from being beautiful, easy, and exciting to routine, difficult, and a chore.

Communication was always a major component of my relationships and I wanted to make sure my wife knew how I was feeling. Unfortunately, communication was an area that Chaun struggled with and expressing herself did not always come easy. Our intimacy was fading and that is a major way that I stay connected with my partner. I had told Chaun multiple times that I was not being satisfied and I needed sex more than once a month or every other month. She had claimed she heard me but nothing was changing and it was only getting worse.

I stared at Chaun across the kitchen table as we ate. I was going to try once again to talk to my wife and express how desperately I needed her.

"I am not getting what I need from you. Is there something wrong?" I asked Chaun.

"What do you mean?" she responded.

With irritation in my voice, "I've told you over and over that I need you. We are not intimate. We've talked about it, I've sent emails about it, we've texted about it, but nothing is changing." I could not believe that she appeared to have no knowledge of what I was speaking about.

"Oh. I don't know. We are just so busy with everything that, you know, it just doesn't happen." she responded nonchalantly.

"Chaun, this has been going on long before all the stuff that we have going on now. Do you remember the calendars?"

We had started keeping track of the number of times we were intimate on a calendar. I wanted to prove to her that the amount of sex we were having was sad. She always tried to make it seem like it was not as bad as I was painting the picture to be. But I wanted to show her that I was not exaggerating and making a big deal out of nothing.

"Yeah I remember them."

"So, I'm going to ask you again. Baby, what's wrong?"

"I don't know. My drive is just off I guess." Chaun said.

"Maybe you need to go to the doctor and see if it is something hormonal. Maybe they can do something to help."

"Yeah. Maybe. I'll talk to Dr. O about it and see what he says"

"But something has to change." I urged her. "I have brought this to you over and over again and you seem like you don't care. I just want you to know that if it doesn't change, I will end up having my needs met somewhere else."

"Ok. We'll figure it out. But if it is that serious for you then maybe you will have to do that."

"Remember you said that. You are going to learn to listen. But just know that I miss you. I want you. Baby I can't tell you enough that I need you and this is one of the ways I feel connected in our relationship. It is not everything but it is a major part for me." I said as I got up from the table and went upstairs.

Nothing ever changed. I had to redirect my focus anyway to dive deep into planning and preparing to open my business. I spent countless hours and many sleepless nights writing and revising my business plan, studying for various licensing exams, and completing hours of online training. It was brutal but it gave me something else I could focus my attention on indirectly filling the void I had with my wife.

I had to show my leadership that I was competent enough to run my business. The demands were high and the stress even higher. My business consumed me but I was happy to go through it knowing I was able to provide for my wife and take care of her like I promised to do.

Chaun had made the decision to put her career on hold and become my Office Manager. In doing so, I required a lot from her and all the members of my team. I had numerous goals, requirements, and expectations I implemented for the office for us to be able to perform to the best of our ability. The demands from my leadership team were immense and being placed under a microscope to perform was beyond stressful. As a result, when the goals were not met, I would get frustrated with Chaun because she understood the seriousness of the first year of the business. There were times when I did not feel like she was doing everything she could to make sure the business was successful. There was no way that I could be the only one giving 110% to propel this business into success and I had a whole team behind me that included my wife. When those feelings arose, I would voice them to her whenever I needed to express them whether it was in the office, during a team meeting, during our commute, or at home. I required more and I had to have it…no excuses.

"Do you think I am asking for too much?" I asked Wisdom.

I had to talk to my friend so I could try to make sense of it all. I had been practically begging Chaun to be with me and to pay attention to the void I was feeling. There had to be an explanation that I was not getting and maybe she could shed some light on this dark place I was stuck in.

"When it comes to relationships a person can never ask for too much. You ask for what you need and what you feel you deserve." she responded.

"But do you think that I am being unreasonable?"

"Absolutely not. Every person is different and what may make one person happy may not work for the next. People want to feel loved, appreciated, and wanted. If you are not receiving that it doesn't make Chaun a bad person and it doesn't make you a bad person either." Wisdom said.

"I get that. But there has to be more to the story. Honestly, I know there is. I just can't prove it."

Wisdom looked at me with a look on her face as though she was waiting for the end of the sentence that had not come yet.

"Go on." She said to me.

"I just feel like Chaun is cheating on me."

"Because of the lack of sex?" she quizzed.

"I mean if she is not giving it to me then she has to be giving it to someone, right?"

"Are you looking for validation or are you legitimately looking for an answer?"

"An answer."

"No, it does not automatically mean that. But you know your wife. You have told me before that you feel like you know her better than she knows herself. So, I can't really answer that for you." Wisdom responded.

I was not truly satisfied with this answer but I had to take it for what it was worth.

"So, am I just supposed to go on in this relationship and sacrifice what I really want because I am in love with her?"

"I think you two have lost sight on what's important." Wisdom responded

"How is that an answer to my question." I retorted.

"It's not. No one can give you the answer to that question. But what I want you to think about is that you two have lost sight on one another. You're focused on your business. From what you say, it seems like her attention is divided. You two have lost sight on one another. You stopped fostering and feeding the relationship."

I hated Wisdom but I loved her at the same time. She always said what needed to be said and what was right. The issue is, it was not always what I wanted to hear. Chaun and I had lost sight on one another. We stopped feeding each other. She stopped giving me what I needed and in turn I did the same. Then the cycle continued. We were both crying out for something and the other person was so consumed with what they were lacking and other outside factors that we failed to pay attention to the other.

The breakdown was immense. Several questions were apparent. Could it be saved or was it too late? Would we be able to redirect our attention and gain our focus back? Was the damage too great? How long was I prepared to continue to be starved in my marriage? I guess only time would tell.

"Happiness and longevity come from being the partner you expect to receive. Show up and give 100% and you in turn will receive the same."

- Candy

CHAPTER
Seven

Trust God for What You Want

We were getting settled into our life together after getting married, relocating, buying our second home, obtaining our MBAs, me being a business owner and Chaun helping to run the business, and having amazing friends and family. There was still one thing that we had dreamt of that we still had not gotten a chance to achieve. We wanted to be parents. Chaun had attempted to conceive years before and was unsuccessful in doing so. Her becoming a mother was something she had wanted for years, even before we ever met. I knew how much this meant to her and knew how disappointed and hurt she was behind not being able to conceive.

My desire and my goal in life was to always give Chaun any and everything she ever desired. I found joy in caring for and providing for my wife. That was a promise that I made to her before, during, and after we were married and I meant that with every fiber of my being. After Chaun had attempted to conceive in the past and was unable to, I made the ultimate decision to try to have our baby. I loved her enough to carry our child. I was nervous but with my faith and Chaun's support, I knew I was able to do it.

After doing days of research we found a fertility specialist we wanted to work with and began the process. We were extremely afraid and nervous of the outcome of the fertility process. We prayed and believed in God but at the same time we had no idea if the kids would be healthy or not. At the end of the day, we were having a child with someone we did not know and had never met. There was an extensive profile and medical history provided for the person but everything that was presented could have been a lie.

Selecting the "perfect" donor seemed like the most life altering decision. We spent weeks scouring through the numerous nameless profiles trying to make sense of it all. All we had to rely on was information provided by the donor that was reminiscent of a personality profile for a dating site and a medical history like the familial background you give to your primary care physician for the first time. How do you choose the "perfect" person with no physical person to go with the information you have? It is more of a leap of faith than anything. But, after pouring over everything we decided on the profile we were most comfortable with and we are happy that we chose who we did.

The donor we choose was Mexican, 6'2" tall, and was described by the staff as "tall, dark, and handsome". It was cliché but we trusted what was provided. I strongly wanted a donor with height considering I am only 5'3" and I was forward thinking. I wanted to give my son an opportunity to be a decent height if I was blessed to conceive and it was a boy. In addition to that, he was in graduate school for Engineering which was an indication to us that he was intelligent. He also had a clean medical history and so did his family. There was also an indication of longevity when it came to his family's life spans. Considering all these factors is what assisted us in making the decision to choose him.

I had to undergo tests, a procedure, and fertility drugs to prepare for our insemination. I needed support through all of this and Chaun was there every step of the way. She only missed one appointment because she had to be in the business for me. We were told there was only a ten to twenty percent chance of conception on the first round of IUI (intrauterine insemination). Also, on average, it takes three to four cycles to conceive. To increase our chances, we made the choice to do two inseminations on back to back days when the time was right.

After doing both inseminations I leaned on my faith in God. I found myself standing in the shower and a sense of peace came over me. I prayed to God and let all my true feelings come out. I expressed how strong my desire to be a mother was and I knew that only He could make it happen if it was my time. Despite being alone, I still allowed myself to be completely vulnerable and share how afraid I was. I knew financially we may not be able to carry on with the three or four cycles we were told it normally took in order to successfully conceive. Tears began to stream down my face and mix with the water as it rained down on me. I laid it all out there and then left it in God's hands. There was nothing more I could do.

Before leaving the shower, I placed my hands on my stomach and simply said, "It is so."

My thirtieth birthday was the following week and Chaun had planned a trip to Miami months ago for us to be able to celebrate. It was both of our first times visiting Miami and we were very excited to be going together. It was a much-needed break for both of us after completing the first year of business and me successfully hitting the goals needed in order to be able to solidify my business. I did not know everything Chaun had planned for me during our trip but I was taking every precaution in case the insemination had been successful and I was pregnant. I did not want to drink any alcohol when we went out and remained very cognizant of everything around me. I remember feeling like I was pregnant and even telling Chaun. But she dismissed it as just being side effects of the fertility medicine and urged me to not get my hopes up high as she did the times she attempted to conceive.

After returning from our trip, I could not shake the feeling that I was pregnant. I felt like I was very much so in tune with my body. I was feeling things I had never felt before and it seemed like much more than just a reaction to the fertility medications. Even though we were instructed not to test before two weeks had passed, I decided to take a home pregnancy test. Chaun was downstairs in the kitchen cooking and I went into our bathroom. After following the instructions, I sat and waited the few minutes, which felt like an eternity, to see what the result was. As I sat on the edge of the tub, I retreated into prayer. In my praying I found myself thanking God before I even knew what the answer was. When I looked at that test and saw the two little lines I was elated. I immediately ran downstairs to Chaun with test in hand.

"I told you there was something to this thing!" I exclaimed.

"What is it babe?"

I handed Chaun the test and she looked at it. A smile spread across her face.

"Are you serious?" she said excitedly.

"Yes."

She was so excited. She danced around the island and ran over and started talking to my stomach.

"Hi little one!"

"We still have to wait for the blood test with the doctor. But I knew I felt like I was pregnant. And I could not get enough of those Checkers fries when we were in Miami."

We both laughed and enjoyed the moment.

The time to visit the doctor for the blood test had finally arrived. It is astonishing how long two weeks can be when you are waiting to get results of something that could change your entire life. We arrived at the specialists office and the typical routine was completed...weight, blood pressure, and temperature. We sat in the room happily chatting while we waited for the nurse to come and draw the blood sample because we felt we already knew the answer. At this point, this was just the logistics that had to be completed in the process. The nurse came and drew the sample and told us to go have lunch because they would be calling us in a few hours with the results. Chaun and I were so excited there was no way we could go into the office and work.

"Thank you for calling. This is Maria. How can I help you?" my front desk team member answered the phone in my office.

"Hey Maria. Chaun and I are not going to be in the office today. How is everything going?"

"Good! Is everything ok?" she asked.

"Yes. Everything is amazing. We just have some things we need to take care of. If you need anything you can call or text us." I said.

We did not want to share with our team what was going on just yet because we wanted to make sure the results are positive and make it through the first trimester. We had heard of unfortunate situations where mothers had shared their awesome news at a time where doctors would say it was too early and then they tragically lost their little angels. That is of course devastating to the parents but can also be difficult for their friends and family as well. Therefore, we had a plan to wait until we made it through the first trimester when the probability of a successful pregnancy was greater.

We made the hour and a half drive back to our suburb of Chicago. We decided on a restaurant to go eat so we could past the time until we heard back from the doctor's office. I kept looking at my phone as if that would make it ring faster than what was going to happen. Just as we had gotten our beverages and placed our order for our food the much-anticipated call came through. I put the phone on speaker so Chaun could hear the news when I heard it.

"Congratulations mommies to be! You're having a baby!" the nurse beamed through the phone.

During the conversation we confirmed the pregnancy and we also received some even more interesting news. There was a high probability that it was going to be a multiple birth because of my hormone levels. It was too soon to tell but once I had my first ultrasound, they would be able to check and confirm.

After speaking with the nurse, Chaun reached out to one of her friends who had also went through the process and had twins to ask her what her levels were. We wanted to see if my levels were like hers. I had a feeling it was twins because twin births ran deep through my family. We counted at least eight sets of twins in my family. Her friend's levels were about half of what mine were and she thought we would be having quadruplets with that high of a reading. All we could think about was "John and

Kate Plus 8" when we heard that news and wondered what in the world we would do with triplets or quadruplets.

We anxiously awaited the ultrasound appointment. In the weeks leading up to the appointment we had run through numerous hypotheticals if we had triplets or quadruplets. We thought about how our lives would change, what that would mean for the business, and what that would mean for us. As might be expected, I leaned back on my faith and I knew God would not give us more than we could handle. So, no matter what the outcome was I was confident we were going to be fine.

When we went to the ultrasound appointment, we were able to confirm that it was going to be twins. I thanked God for not only answering my prayer for one healthy baby but honoring us with two little precious gifts. Up until then, my pregnancy had been a breeze. I was able to continue my day to day routine and continue running my business without skipping a beat.

However, about a week later, I started to get very sick. It started to get very difficult for me to eat and keep food down. Initially we were not too alarmed because we attributed it to morning sickness. We researched remedies to help with my nausea and tried to gauge how long it would last. Everything we found estimated I should be better once I made it through the first trimester so I endured it thinking there was a light at the end of the tunnel.

My first trimester concluded but the sickness did not. Not only did it not subside but it was progressively getting worse. Barely anything I ate would stay down. I began to become miserable, afraid, and sad. My ability to go into my business was dwindling. As my pregnancy progressed, Chaun had to assist me sometimes with things that were everyday tasks. I would find myself praying to God that he would keep me and allow me to make it through this experience. My sadness and despair increased to the point where I became depressed and did not want to leave the house anymore.

There were literally times I did not think I would make it through my pregnancy. At my checkup appointments I informed my doctor of what I was going through and she finally put a label on it, Hyperemesis Gravidarum. Again, I was given an estimate of when things should get better which was around twenty weeks of the pregnancy. Unfortunately, twenty weeks came and went but the sickness did not. It was so bad that my doctor often presented the option of terminating the pregnancy. But I could never choose that because I had to trust God and I knew these two little babies that I was birthing were important and this was greater than me.

By my third trimester my doctor prescribed me anti-nausea medication for me to be able to keep some food down because I had gained minimal weight up to that point which was a concern. I finally had relief, albeit it was nominal at best, it still gave me the ability to eat a little bit and be able to keep it down. But having to take medicine every time I wanted to eat or drink something was concerning so I kept it to a minimum. As my due date grew near, I had additional difficulties coupled on top of the sickness. My joints began to ache, I had difficulty sleeping, my feet and ankles were so swollen I had to resort to wearing Jordan sandals and socks in the winter, and my depression held steady.

In the last month of my pregnancy I was now being seen weekly by my doctor. Every week I was practically begging the doctor to schedule the C-section so I could end the misery I was in. Each time I was told my vitals were good, the babies vitals were strong, and the longer I could keep the babies in, the healthier they would be when they arrived. I had to constantly put myself on the backburner and keep the babies' best interest in the forefront of my mind.

Thankfully I made it through and we were blessed with two beautiful babies on November 19, 2013. But the challenges carried through all the way up to the moment our little angels arrived. When it was time for my C-section to take place, I was wheeled into the operating room so they could prep me before allowing Chaun to join me. While I was being prepped I heard commotion in the room but I was not really able to tell what was going on because I was strapped down with IVs running into my arm, oxygen in my nose, and a sheet draped across my chest blocking my view of the doctor and the surgical team on the other side. I could feel myself slipping out of consciousness and my blood pressure had begun to drop. My initial instinct was to go to God. As I felt myself slipping, I asked God to see me through and to allow my babies to be born healthy. Right before everything went completely black, I can remember saying, "It is so".

The next thing I knew I felt a nurse close to my face asking me to say my name and asking me if I knew where I was. Once I was able to answer her questions, I felt better and they were bringing Chaun in the room. She was outfitted in green scrubs, a medical mask, and a surgical cap. I was so happy to see her because she had been with me every step of the way since conception and I knew I could not have done this without her.

Moments later Kennedy and Kayleb arrived completely healthy and our family was complete. Tears streamed down our faces as we welcomed our baby girl and our baby boy. The nurses held them close to my face so I could kiss them before they took them to the nursery to perform all the tests and additional things they do for newborns. I told Chaun to go be with our babies because I wanted her to stay with them until they were brought to me in the recovery room.

Through it all one thing was certain, I trusted God and His process. There were times when I questioned if I was strong enough and whether I had made the right decision but this moment made it all worth it. At the beginning of this journey, if I could see around the corner, I would have been too afraid to take a step. But I guess that is why life is set up the way it is, we are not meant to see the future for that very reason. As we go through life and its challenges, we are taught that we are 100% stronger than we ever imagined ourselves to be. A journey of a thousand miles starts with one step. Have faith, believe in yourself, and face your fears with confidence and determination.

"Trust God and His process. We are not meant to see around the corner because it could petrify us. You are 100% stronger than you ever imagined yourself to be."

- Candy

CHAPTER

Eight

Infidelity Is Almost A Certainty

haun and I were now at a point where we seemingly had it all. On paper we were the model couple. We had the home, business, marriage, twins, family, and friends. What more could anyone ask for? Well, there was a major part of the puzzle that was missing. After Kennedy and Kayleb, who we affectionately began to call KenKay, arrived, Chaun and I immersed ourselves into caring for two tiny babies. They became our priority with my business following closely second. The same issue I had been begging, communicating, and pleading with Chaun about for over two years was still very much so present. The distance, lack of intimacy, and lack of communication I had pointed out continued to grow. The very thing I cautioned Chaun about over a year ago came to fruition…I had an affair.

Nya was a former coworker of me and Chaun's from years prior. After Chaun and I had left the company we saw Nya on occasion when visiting a friend who lived near her. But there was never a connection between her and I. I never viewed her as anything more than a coworker and quite frankly, I did not even know she was attracted to women, let alone me. Nya and I reconnected on social media some years after Chaun and I had relocated.

I randomly received a friend request on Facebook one day from Nya and of course I accepted it because I recognized who she was. After accepting the friend request, I did not think anything else about it. After the request came an inbox message. Nya had reached out and wanted to know how Chaun and I had been doing. She admitted having watched our lives unfold on Facebook. She had seen when I proposed, the wedding pictures, when we relocated, the start of my business, the baby shower, and the birth of our twins. It was as if she was reading a manuscript to a movie that she was excited to learn more about. But of course, there was a lot that was not depicted in those happy and memorable Facebook posts.

As time went on, Nya and I began to communicate more and more. It was refreshing for me to have a friend that I could talk to that really seemed genuinely interested in what I had to say. It got to the point where our communication increased to being daily and we talked off and on through the day. Chaun was completely aware that I was talking to Nya and we even offered for her to come and visit us one weekend since it had been years since we had all seen one another. We decided we were all going to go out and have a night out in Chicago.

Unfortunately, when the weekend came, the babysitter we had previously secured was unable to watch the twins for us.

"We can all just hang out at the house then. I know how it is with kids." Nya said to us.

"No. You did not come all this way to sit in the house." Chaun said laughing.

"Yeah but I am fine with that." Nya said.

"Not at all. You and Candy go and have a good time. I can stay here with the babies." Chaun insisted.

"Baby are you sure?" I asked.

"Positive."

Nya and I got dressed to go out. We went and had a good time that night. After that weekend I found myself becoming more and more comfortable with talking to Nya. I got to the point where I started confiding in Nya about the issues I was having in my marriage. She listened attentively and without judgment. One thing you must be cautious about when sharing difficulties about your relationship is depending on who is listening, that same information can be used in a way to give you what you are missing and what you are yearning for. Yet, hindsight is 20/20 and I appreciated having someone to listen. I let Nya in on the lack of intimacy I had been experiencing for years and how I had a strong desire to feel wanted. I missed how Chaun once looked at me like I was the most important person in the world. Chaun used to make me feel like her world was incomplete without me in it. Those feelings had faded and I felt like more of an obligation than a desired partner.

"I hate to hear you say that." Nya said.

"I hate to have to say it. It has been such a long time and I just don't understand what I can do to make it better."

"I am not sure but you are a beautiful woman. You provide for your family, you have your own business, I see how hard you love. Any woman would want what Chaun has."

I think it was in that moment that I started to feel a shift in me and Nya's relationship. I noticed that she began to say things that made me feel good again and made my confidence level rise again. The friendly texts started to shift in a different direction. They went from "Good morning. I hope you had a good night" to "Good morning. I miss you". The conversations also began to become flirtatious and sexual in nature. I knew deep down inside this was wrong but it was like someone else was in control of me. Sometimes you have no idea how much you have been starved until you are fed again. I was drawn to the attention, affection, and desire Nya had for me like a bee to a marigold. It seemed like everything Nya said was exactly what I needed to hear.

This communication continued for a few weeks and the next move I made was the crucial one that changed our relationship forever. My text message alert sounded and I picked my phone up.

Hey boo. I miss you. I am having a few friends over on Saturday. I would love for you to come down and hang out with us.

I read the message from Nya. I sat and contemplated this for a little while before responding. Something inside of me knew that if I went to see her our relationship would move on to another level based on the conversations we had been having. I had the opportunity then to make a key decision that could alter my life and potentially jeopardize my marriage. At that moment I should have responded "No. I think I'll pass" and have a conversation with Nya to let her know we can no longer have inappropriate conversations and go back to the platonic level we were once on. Instead, I picked up my phone and responded.

Hey bae. I miss you too. I'm there. I can't wait to see you."

I let Chaun know that Nya had invited me to hang out with her and some friends on Saturday night. I never asked her if she wanted to go and was hoping she would not ask. With a sigh of relief, she never asked to join me. I had so many thoughts running through my head as Saturday approached. I was literally in turmoil with myself. There were a couple of times where I almost changed my mind but I decided to continue. As I made the hour and a half drive to Nya's house, I tried to convince myself that nothing was going to happen.

I never thought I would be in this position in my marriage where I was considering being with another woman. Because if I was honest with myself, Chaun was still the one and only woman I wanted. She was my first choice...my only choice. But you can only plead your case for so long and not be heard before you begin to seek what you are missing elsewhere. I pulled into the parking lot of Nya's apartment complex and turned my truck off. I stared at myself in the rearview mirror. What I saw in my eyes was the look of a woman hurt, angry, and frustrated. I had come all this way so I might as well continue down the path.

Nya greeted me with open arms. She hugged me and the hug seemed to linger just past the point of just being friends. I remember smelling her perfume and feeling the softness of her skin and I knew right then I had gotten to the point of no return. The night continued with her friends. I found a comfortable place to sit while everyone else was drinking, dancing to the music, and playing cards. Nya continuously checked on me to make sure I was ok and that I did not want anything to drink or eat. She catered to my every need. The only time I had to get up was if I had to use the bathroom. Even in a room full of people, I felt like I was the only person that mattered to her. The feeling of being wanted and needed flared up inside of me.

The night went on and slowly the guests began to dissipate. It was late but I still could have made the drive home and saved myself. But I chose to stay. The last person left leaving me and Nya there alone. We sat on the couch and we continued talking and laughing for a while. Then as if a scene from a movie was being played out, the conversation ceased and we began kissing. The intensity and desire that exuded from her was powerful.

"I have been wanting you so bad." she said softly between kisses.

"How bad do you want me?" I asked with a bit of ego in my voice.

"Bad enough to invite you down for a random house party hoping that you'll do exactly what you're doing now."

She took my hand and slid it underneath her shirt. I massaged her breasts and her breathing got heavy. Hearing her made me excited and I wanted more. This was another chance for me to change gears but my carnal nature took over and the next couple of hours were spent in Nya's bedroom exchanging blissful moments. I got lost in the lust and the desire. As we laid there afterwards, I knew at that moment I had spun the wheel of deception and my marriage would never be the same.

We sat up talking for a few more hours and I saw the sun begin to rise. I knew I had to return home. I took a quick shower and kissed Nya goodbye.

"Bye baby. Let me know when you make it home safe." she said as she rolled over and headed back to sleep.

"I will. Text me when you get up."

As I walked to my truck, I had a sinking feeling in my stomach. The night before played in my head over and over. I had conflicting emotions running through me as I made my way down the highway. Would Chaun notice anything different? Would I be able to keep this secret in? What was I going to do next? Was it really such a bad thing since I had warned Chaun years ago that I would get my needs met elsewhere if things did not improve? I rationalized with the idea that what she does not know cannot hurt her. I was in a state of turmoil but at the same time I was filled with adrenaline and excitement.

When I returned home Chaun was up dealing with the twins. She greeted me like normal and a sense of relief came over me. I was safe. I showered again and fell into our normal Sunday routine of caring for the twins, helping to clean the house, and prepare for my week of work. All the while I held my cell phone close to me so I could continue to communicate with Nya who had begun texting me as soon as she woke up.

You felt so good last night. I miss you already. When can I see you again?

Message after message came through and I fought to keep a straight face and not smile like I wanted to so I could keep down any suspicions or questions Chaun may have if she witnessed it on my face. It is amazing how a state of paranoia can come over you when you have a secret of that magnitude to hide.

As soon as you want. When is the next time you can take a day off? I can come see you while Chaun is at work.

By this time, Chaun had left my business and was working somewhere else. This made it easier for me to come and go without her knowledge. The affair grew to the point where I was traveling to see Nya two to three times a week. I had the timing down to a science. I would leave right after Chaun and the twins left for the day. I would spend those days talking, laughing, and, of course, having sex, and I would leave with enough time to make sure I would make it home before Chaun and the twins would arrive. Some days I would even leave a little early and pick the twins up for Chaun to lighten her load from time to time. The level of adrenaline and excitement was intoxicating. I think I even became a little addicted to it. Being able to do what was forbidden and not get caught.

Eventually, I think I must have become so wrapped up in Nya that Chaun became suspicious. I do not know if it was a situation of me becoming careless and not covering my tracks as well or if I had gotten to the point where subconsciously I did not care if Chaun knew or found out. Nya was my safe haven, my place of peace, and the source of my sexual gratification. Nya and I did things sexually that Chaun and I had not done in years or had never done. I was free with her. I almost felt like I was free to do what I wanted with her because she was not my wife and maybe in some sick twisted way, I did not have to give her the same level of respect as I would my wife. Whatever the reason, I was hooked and could not get enough. It had gotten to the point where I stopped really craving Chaun anymore since I was being satisfied so well with Nya.

One day while me, Chaun, and the twins were at my grandmother's house visiting, my world came crashing in on me. Earlier that week I had told Chaun I was taking my grandmother to a dentist appointment. This was just a clever ruse to cover up one of my many trips to see Nya. While we all set around talking and playing with the twins my grandmother inadvertently let the cat out of the bag.

"So, Candy I forgot to tell you what happened when I went to the dentist the other day." my grandmother exclaimed.

My heart literally sank and I immediately looked at Chaun. If I could have found a hole to crawl into at that moment I would have and never resurfaced. I carried on with the conversation with my grandmother and tried to change the subject as quickly as possible. While amid the conversation, I quickly grabbed my phone and sent a message to Chaun.

Baby I love you.

I saw her grab her phone and read the message I sent. Her fingers moved quickly across the screen and my phone buzzed.

I love you too. But clearly, we need to talk.

I knew after this visit it was going to be a long night. I was panicking inside and had no idea what to do or say. Our visit lasted for about another hour and I could feel the tension from Chaun as we packed the kids up so we could head home. As we rode home the looming conversation began.

"I am guessing you did not take your grandmother to the dentist like you said." Chaun began.

"No." I replied, not wanting to give too much information and allow Chaun to lead the conversation in the hopes it would not go as far as I was dreading.

"Where were you then?" she probed.

"We don't really need to have this conversation." I said trying to derail this train.

"What do you mean we don't need to have this conversation?"

"Because. What is it really going to prove?"

"Are you sleeping with her?" Chaun quizzed.

"Who?"

I could see her looking at me from my peripheral. Her eyes were piercing through me like knives. I was feeling nauseous now and just wanted this to be over.

"You can't handle me telling you that." I said,

"I've seen the messages. I know it is more than friends. Are you fucking her?" Chaun hissed.

"What do you mean you've seen the messages? Have you been going through my phone?" I asked pissed.

"Yes. So, are you going to tell the truth now?" she fired back now with tears slowly running down her face.

I had pulled into a gas station to get gas and knew I needed to get some air. I was so angry at the fact that she had violated my privacy and had been going through my phone. Yet, this was when the rubber was meeting the road. It is true that every choice and decision has consequences so now it was time for me to face the consequences of my actions. I placed the gas pump back in its holster, took a deep breath, and got back in the truck.

"To answer your question, yes. I am having sex with her. Considering you don't want to and I brought it to you multiple times." I said with anger filling my words.

"This is my fault?" Chaun quizzed.

"I made myself perfectly clear when I kept bringing my needs to you. I begged and pleaded with you. I told you if things didn't get better, I would get what I needed from somewhere else. But this was not done in an effort to hurt you. I didn't even know it was going to happen. I wasn't looking for it."

Chaun did not say anything else in the truck. After we got home and put the twins down for bed, we spent hours talking and crying. I could not release the feeling of rejection, disappointment, frustration, and anger I was feeling behind everything that had occurred. Thinking about what led us here made me sick to my stomach.

Over the next six months my affair with Nya continued. Chaun had all the information she needed to make the decision that was best for her. She made the decision to stay in our marriage and try to deal with the knowledge of knowing I was seeing someone else. When Nya found out Chaun knew about us she was nervous but trusted my lead. I still respected Chaun and my time with her was with her. Conversely, my time with Nya was with her.

Nya and I dealt with a level of guilt knowing what we were doing. However, at the same time, the love and affection I was receiving from Nya kept me going back. I had also grown close to her children. I talked to them about issues they were having at school, assisted Nya with disciplinary tactics, and encouraged them.

As I continued to deal with the emotions of two women, my own conflicting feelings, and the highs and lows the affair had on my marriage, I was getting to the point where I felt like I wanted to end things with Nya. I knew I was still in love with Chaun and that took precedence over my feelings for Nya. I loved and cared for her but how long could I continue living like this? I had always told Nya that I would never leave Chaun.

"This situation is getting the best of me, Wisdom." I confided in my friend.

"Then it sounds like you have a decision to make." Wisdom responded matter of fact.

"But how do I make a decision like this. Chaun has changed and begun to show me more attention but how do I know it's not just because she knows someone else is giving it to me now?"

Chaun had started to cater to me and began to give me the things I had been begging for over the years. But it seemed very odd to me that I was getting it now that I had strayed. Why now when someone else was willing and able to give me what I was starving for?

"Have you asked her?" Wisdom asked.

"Asked her what?" I inquired.

"Whether or not the changes are genuine or if it is just because she feels threatened by Nya."

"No. But who would really admit to that? If she admitted it was only because of Nya then that would be saying she is lying about her intentions." I said.

"But you'll never know. You should at least have the conversation to see." Wisdom insisted.

I did end up mentioning it to Chaun and she did admit that she took me for granted. She said she never thought I would carry out stepping outside of our marriage. However, her actions were genuine and she had always loved me. There was still something inside of me that was not sure about her intentions. Yet, I had to accept what she said and move on. I made the decision to work on my marriage. I wanted my wife even after everything that had happened.

I had started to pull away from Nya and I think she could sense the distance. She began to ask what was wrong and why things were changing. Chaun was on her way home so I knew I did not have much time to have the conversation, but I had to let it be known.

"Nya, I can't do this anymore. I want my marriage and if I am going to make it work, I have to focus on my wife. Only my wife. I love you but I can't continue this."

There was silence on the other end of the phone. I sat there quietly for a moment but knew I had to let her go before Chaun arrived.

"Did you hear what I said?" I broke the silence.

"You said you loved me. Everything was fine." Nya said. I could hear the crack in her voice and could tell she was fighting back tears.

"I do love you. But I am in love with my wife and that is what I want." I insisted.

"I want my key back since you can just walk away like this." She snapped.

"That's fine. But I have to go." I said quickly and hung up the phone.

Moments later, Chaun was coming in the door. I took Chaun into the TV room and let her know I wanted to talk. The whole time Nya was texting and calling my phone nonstop. I ignored every message and rejected every call. I could not believe she was doing this knowing Chaun was home and after what I had just told her. She had never disrespected the boundaries I put on our relationship. She knew when to contact me and when not to. But it seemed like this moment of finality was too much for her. I knew it was not going to be easy for her but I never thought she would go this far.

"Baby I'll be right back. I'm about to go shower really quick since the twins are sleep. When I come back, I want to talk to you." I said to Chaun as I hurried upstairs.

I had to try to get Nya under control and give her something so she would calm down. She continued sending message after message.

You will not keep ignoring me. If you don't respond to me and give me my key back, I will be at your door.

I could not believe she was threatening me. It has always been said if you play with fire then you will get burned. I was starting to feel the heat from the fire getting close.

Do not threaten me. I told you I will give you your key back. This is not the time to talk right now. Chaun is home and I will contact you later. Do not respond.

Nya was relentless and continued to call and text. I showered quickly and went back to Chaun who was still sitting in the TV room. I sat down and let Chaun know I had ended things with Nya. I let her know I was in love with her and that I wanted our marriage. I assured her that she was always who I wanted and I apologized for hurting her. As we were sitting there talking, Chaun's phone began to ring. I could not believe my eyes, it was Nya.

"Do you want to take this?" Chaun asked.

"No. Don't answer it." I responded.

Chaun let the call go to voicemail. Then my phone rang. Nya again. I did not answer. I informed Chaun what was going on and why she was calling the way she was.

"If she calls again, I am going to answer." Chaun hissed.

My mind was in a whirlwind. Just then, my phone rang again. Chaun swiftly grabbed my phone and answered.

"Hello."

"Who is this?" Nya said.

"What do you mean 'who is this?'" Chaun snapped back.

"Put Candy on the phone."

"You don't run shit here. She told you it was over so stop calling and texting her phone."

"I want my key back."

"Candy will mail it to you. Now get off the phone!"

Chaun hung up before giving Nya the chance to say anything in return.

I had never seen Chaun like this before. The way she took control and stood her ground was attractive. My phone grew silent and I noticed the time. I had to leave to pick up my mom who was going to be watching the kids while Chaun and I went out later that night to a friend's comedy show.

On our way back to the house I filled my mom in on what had happened. I needed someone to talk to about it and my mom could tell something was bothering me. My mom just listened and shook her head.

"You are your daddy's child." she said jokingly.

As I pulled closer to the house, I saw a familiar black SUV sitting in front of my house. This could not be happening. I did not want to believe what I was seeing. Nya was sitting in front of my house in her vehicle, waiting. I pulled into my driveway and let the garage door up. I pulled my truck in and let my mom out. I told her to go inside and keep Chaun and KenKay inside. I approached Nya feeling the ultimate level of betrayal from her. Nya and I exchanged words in the driveway and I gave her apartment key back to her. I hoped this would be the end of it. But Nya continued, yelling at me from the end of the driveway.

"You can't do this to me! You said you loved me!" Nya screamed.

"Girl, stop! It's over."

"You are such a fucking liar!" she screamed back.

Chaun surfaced from the front door and came out on to the porch. My mom and the twins were standing in the doorway looking on.

"If you don't take your ghetto ass out from in front of my house. We don't do that here." Chaun said with authority trying not to be too loud.

"Don't tell me what to do. Go back in the house. This has nothing to do with you." Nya yelled back.

Chaun lurched forward and my mom grabbed her and took her back in the house.

"Get in your truck and leave, Nya. You are dead to me." I said to Nya as I walked in the house and closed the garage door.

My love for Nya died that day in the driveway. This was the ultimate disrespect. Not only did she disrespect me but she brought drama to my front door. She disrespected herself, my wife, my mother and my children. I knew I was completely done. There was no turning back. I would miss the positive attributes of Nya but this display at my house showed me a little glimpse of crazy that I was not willing to take any chances with ever again.

Chaun and I attempted to move forward but we never did the appropriate work on the relationship that would have been necessary for us to fully move forward. Within no time, I was back to feeling rejected and the lack of intimacy became all too familiar. Little would I know that when Chaun and I went to the comedy show that night this would be the beginning of my second affair.

> *"If a relationship is not cultivated, infidelity will almost be a certainty. Pay attention, take heed to what your partner is communicating, and be prepared to do the work."*
>
> *- Candy*

CHAPTER
Nine

The Other Woman

After the Nya debacle at my home, I had

decided that I was returning to being all in with my marriage. I knew there had been a lot of damage done on both sides, but if I was going to try to make it work, I was going to have to refocus and channel my energy back into my wife. We talked again as we made our way to the comedy show that night. I apologized for hurting her and bringing drama to our home. I never thought me having my physical needs met somewhere else could bring strife and turmoil to my life.

Going out that night was a breath of fresh air after the events which unfolded earlier in the day. We reconnected with friends from college to support our guy Derrick who was making a name for himself in the comedy and entertainment world. Jalisa had invited Chaun and I to come out since she had come to town to support Derrick. Derrick was Jalisa's daughter's father and they had fostered an amazing friendship with one another after they split years ago.

"Hi Candace!" Jalisa squealed as she jumped out of the car she was sitting in. "I am so glad to see you!"

I hugged Jalisa tight and was so happy to see her.

"Hey baby!" I exclaimed while hugging her.

"Oh my God! You cut your hair?! It looks so good on you." she said.

Jalisa had not seen me since I had cut my hair short. We stood there chit chatting for a few moments when Tamia stepped out of the car. Tamia was Jalisa's sorority sister and I knew her from college as well. We had run in the same social circles but never really knew much about one another.

"Hey Mia. How have you been?" I said to Tamia and gave her a hug.

Mia was what she was always known as. No one called her by her full name. I was even introduced to her as Mia in college when Jalisa first introduced me to her. Mia was always quiet in comparison to Jalisa who was outspoken and could take a room by storm with her bubbly personality. But one thing that always stood out to me about Mia was her smile. Even if she did not say a word, her smile would light up the room.

"Good. How have you been? You look good." she answered.

"Good. Mia this is my wife Chaun."

"Nice to meet you." Chaun beamed.

We went inside and had an amazing time at the comedy show. Afterwards Jalisa said she was in town for a couple more days and wanted to get together again so we could catch up. The next day I met Jalisa at her mom's house so we could hang out. Mia was there as well. It was funny because I had seen her so many times in the past but had never actually saw her. She was 5'7" with a beautiful mocha skin tone and a body that could bring a man, or woman, to her knees. She was gorgeous. How had I never noticed this before?

The even funnier thing was she had been the same person that accompanied Jalisa to me and Chaun's wedding. During that visit my interaction with Mia changed. I am not sure how or why it happened, but there was a shift in our dynamic. We flirted back and forth with one another which really surprised me because I had never known her to be attracted to women. I found out she lived in Chicago and we exchanged numbers so we could reconnect. That day was the beginning and the end for me in many ways. A simple exchange of phone numbers between two old college acquaintances would change my life in a way I never knew.

Mia and I began texting after that day exchanging long conversations. I shared with her things about Nya. Mia was like a sounding board for me during the times when I missed Nya. She gave me the strength to not reach out to Nya during those moments when I was weak and wanted to reach out to her again. But the more I talked to Mia, the less I thought about Nya. Mia became my antidote to the poison that was coursing through me called Nya. It got to the point where I stopped thinking about her and Mia began to fill my thoughts. She was smart, funny, intense, intelligent, and sassy.

It got to the point where texting was no longer enough. We wanted to see each other face to face and spend time with each other. So, for a couple of weeks I would sneak to go to Mia's house in Chicago. For Chaun, I was going to business meetings. I do not really know why I started off with the dishonesty, but I guess it was because I knew I was attracted to Mia and had a feeling I was going back down and all too familiar path I had just recently escaped with Nya. Our visits transformed from lunches and dinners to me spending entire days at her house and us having sex during the breaks between her meetings when she worked from home.

Her soft chocolate skin and voluptuous curves drove me insane. The way she would remove her glasses when she approached me and straddle me on the couch was my invitation to pleasure every time. I would get lost in her for hours. I forgot about the world around me when I was with her. Her lavender fragrance was like its own aphrodisiac when I smelled it.

"What the fuck am I doing?" I asked Wisdom.

"I don't know what to tell you Candy. It seems to me you are still not happy in your marriage. If you were, you wouldn't be in this situation again mere weeks from the last one." she retorted.

"Wow. Tell me how you feel why don't you."

"You know I always will. What are you going to do?" Wisdom asked.

"I don't know because Mia is supposed to come to the house and hang out with Chaun and I. I can't cancel because that would look suspicious but then how am I supposed to bring Mia to the house knowing that we're sleeping with each other?" I said desperately.

"You have a tough decision to make. You could easily end things with Mia and get refocused like you were supposed to or you could continue on and see how it ends."

I was tired of having to make difficult decisions. With this, I decided to just go with my feelings and see how everything goes. I enjoyed being with Mia and the sex was excellent. We were just friends with benefits. There was no harm in that. There were tons of people who did it and Mia knew the entire situation. She said she was just having fun with me so there was no reason to think otherwise. Also, I was in love with Chaun and she was getting past Nya.

Leading up to the weekend Mia was extremely nervous and a little unsure but I convinced her everything was fine.

Candy are you sure I should come to the house this weekend. I mean, how am I supposed to sit in front of Chaun knowing what we've been doing?

I read the text from Mia and knew I had to ease her fears.

She has no idea what's going on. It is fine. Just come here for the weekend. We'll have a good time. Plus, if you don't come it'll raise questions.

A few moments passed with no response from Mia. I texted her again.

Do you trust me?

A few more moments passed and my phone vibrated.

Yes. I trust you. I'll be there.

The impending weekend arrived. Mia arrived Friday night and the festivities began. When she showed up and I opened the door for her my insides instantly stirred. The physical attraction I had for her was immense.

I hugged her tight and whispered in her ear, "I want you so bad. This weekend is going to be torture."

She whispered back, "I feel the same way. You should feel how wet I am."

"Don't make this any harder than it already is."

We broke our connection and I gathered my thoughts.

"Hey Mia." Chaun said when we entered the TV room. "Do you want something to drink?"

"Sure. Can I have some water? I should drink some water before we start drinking the wine I brought" Mia answered holding a bottle of red wine in her hand.

"Nice. Babe, I can make you a daquiri since you don't drink wine." Chaun said to me.

"Thanks babe."

The night began with us ordering food. We ate, talked, and laughed. The night was going awesome and I was in heaven. I had my beautiful wife along with my gorgeous "special" friend. The thoughts that were swirling around in my head were extremely erotic, maybe even downright naughty to some.

"Oooh. I have an idea." Chaun exclaimed. "Let's play Dirty Hearts. It's a great conversation starter."

"I'm game." I answered.

"What's Dirty Hearts?" Mia asked.

"Well, I am not sure if that is really what it's called, but that's what I call it. Basically, you take a deck of cards and you pass them out one at a time. Whoever gets a heart, everyone else gets to ask them a question and you have to answer honestly." Chaun explained.

"Sounds interesting. Let's do it." Mia said.

Chaun went to the kitchen to grab the deck of cards.

"Guess what Chaun." I said.

"What's up?"

"Mia thinks you are sexy." I blurted out. Maybe the daquiri was making my mouth loose.

"Whatever Candy." Chaun said.

"I'm serious." Mia and I chuckled.

"It's true. I've always thought you were attractive." Mia said.

"Really? I didn't even know you were into girls." Chaun said blushing.

Mia sipped her wine and smiled. "Looks like this card game may be more fun than we thought." she said.

Chaun sat down on the floor with the cards and started to pass the cards around. During the game it came out Mia had been with women before, she found Chaun and I attractive, and some other background information was shared. Mia and Chaun shared a few flirtatious remarks back and forth. I was looking at these two sexy women that both excited me in different ways. I picked up my phone and texted Chaun.

I want to see you and Mia together.

Chaun picked up her phone when it buzzed and opened the message. I could see an expression of surprise come over her face and she looked at me. The look in her eyes gave off, "Are you serious?". I smiled at her. She texted me back.

Are you being for real?

I knew Chaun was a little fearful and was also being very cautious because I never could imagine her being with anyone else besides me. Also, knowing that I had suspicions about her fidelity left her wondering if this was a test or a setup to see where her loyalty lied. It was none of those things. I genuinely wanted to see them together and I think in a way, it would make me feel not so guilty for the fact that I had already been sleeping with Mia. I responded to her message.

I am serious.

Chaun read the message and put her phone down. We continued to play the card game. Mia said something else flirtatious.

"You keep it up you are going to find yourself upstairs." Chaun quickly responded.

"Is that right?" Mia said coyly.

"Well let's go." I interjected.

We all looked at one another for a few moments and the next thing I knew we were all making our way upstairs to me and Chaun's master bedroom.

"I need to shower." Chaun said.

"I do too. Can I join you?" Mia asked.

"You sure can."

Mia left the room for a moment to grab her things she needed for the shower.

"Are you sure about this?" Chaun asked while she held my hand.

"Yes baby. I'm sure." I said.

Chaun removed her clothes and we entered our en suite bathroom. I sat on the bathtub and watched Chaun with her caramel skin, long legs, and plump breast step into the shower. A few moments later Mia entered the bathroom. She had pulled her hair up and began to disrobe in front of me. Her smooth dark mocha skin started to appear and I had to ignore my desire to reach out and touch her despite how much I wanted her. She pulled her panties down over her full hips and round ass and I instantly got wet going back to the last time her and I had been together. Mia winked at me as she joined Chaun in the shower.

I sat there watching these two beautiful women in the shower and could not believe what was happening. Mia faced Chaun and began to lather her using her loofa.

"You are beautiful." Mia softly said to Chaun.

"You are too." Chaun responded.

They began to kiss and I thought I was going to explode just by watching them. The show continued with them lathering one another as they caressed each other's breasts, legs, and planted soft kisses on different parts of their bodies. Once they rinsed off, they both exited the shower and we transferred the party into the bedroom. Chaun laid Mia softly down on the bed and I took a seat in our brown leather chair in the corner. I did not want to miss a moment of this display of affection.

Chaun climbed into the bed and straddled Mia. They looked into each other's eyes for a moment. I wondered what was going on in their minds as they locked eyes. I was also trying to determine what was going on with me as well. As I watched them, I knew I was aroused but I also felt another set of emotions creeping in. While Chaun and Mia were enjoying this moment that I instigated, I noticed feelings of jealousy and betrayal started to creep into my psyche. Oddly, it was very erotic and I continued to watch.

"If at any point you want me to stop just let me know." Chaun said to Mia.

"Ok I will."

Chaun softly kissed Mia before making her way down to her breasts. She licked and sucked on her nipples and Mia began to softly moan. She looked over at me and mouthed 'are you ok?'. I shook my head affirmatively. Chaun continued down her body and parted her thighs. I could see how excited Mia had become by the glistening wetness in her center. Chaun began to please her orally and Mia started to move her body with the rhythm Chaun was creating.

As Chaun was pleasing Mia she beckoned me over with her index finger. She wanted me to join to make this a trio rather than a duo. I declined the offer. I wanted to witness them two together. Mia's body started to shutter and I knew she was climaxing. Chaun kept feasting on her as she likes to do. Chaun tends to want to bring you to a level of ecstasy you may have not experienced before. Mia exploded another time.

"Stop. I can't take it." Mia moaned.

Chaun stopped and let Mia up. Mia giggled a little too herself as she got up from the bed

"My legs are weak and I'm sex drunk!" She exclaimed.

We all laughed.

"What is sex drunk?" I asked.

"You know. When you have such a strong orgasm that you feel drunk after you cum. That's what I feel like right now." Mia said as she stood bent over at the foot of the bed.

"I guess I can take that as a compliment." Chaun said

"You absolutely can."

After a moment Mia laid Chaun down on the bed and she reciprocated the pleasure she had received. I watched as Mia explored Chaun's body and my excitement creeped back up again. I enjoyed this seductive exchange between these two beautiful women. That night after Mia retired to our guest room, I made love to Chaun. Yet, a part of me was in the guest room with Mia. I found myself in turmoil but had to deal with it in silence as I could not express my desires with Chaun knowing she had no idea about Mia and me.

After that night, the next ten weeks continued in a very vacillating manner. Mia would regularly come and spend the weekends with us but it came with its share of hurdles that we all had to overcome. There were moments of jealousy, envy, confusion, and betrayal that were experienced by each of us at varying times. Mia got a chance to observe Chaun and I be intimate which she later disclosed made her a little jealous but was erotic at the same time.

The next hurdle was Chaun discovering that Mia and I had been intimate before our first weekend together. That one was difficult and caused issues between all three of us. Chaun was upset that we had lied to her. Mia was upset that I put her in the position to be deceptive. And I was furious that Chaun had went through my phone again which is how she discovered the truth. Yet, despite all the emotions, we made it through it and Chaun advised she would be willing to deal with Mia and I seeing one another.

We shared one more intimate moment together before things began to come to a head. I originally was accepting to the idea of Chaun and Mia building a relationship separate of the three of us. However, I noticed there would be times when Mia and Chaun would be in communication but I would not hear from Chaun and the contact between Mia and I would be lessened. The green-eyed monster crept up on me and I decided to let Mia and Chaun know I was no longer willing to deal with them talking outside the three of us. If I had taken a moment to be honest with myself, I would have been able to admit it was because my feelings for Mia were increasing and I no longer viewed her as just a friend with benefits. She was beginning to be so much more to me.

The final weekend we spent together I noticed that Chaun was standoffish towards Mia. The energy and the atmosphere were completely different from what our normal weekends consisted of. I pulled Chaun to the side and wanted to have a conversation with her because Mia mentioned how uncomfortable she felt.

"What is the issue?" I asked Chaun.

"What do you mean?" she replied.

"Your mood and energy are off. What is going on?"

"I don't know what you are talking about." she said with a little irritation. "I am fine."

"Chaun, come on. You're not being real. Mia feels super uncomfortable and you have been really standoffish."

"Oh. So, you are coming to me because of your precious Mia feels some kind of way. That's cute." she spewed.

"What is that supposed to mean?" I probed.

"It seems to me like you care more about how Mia feels than how I feel."

"I don't know where this is coming from but you are trippin' and you need to get it together." I snapped.

"Why? Because you love her now?" Chaun said.

"What do you mean?"

"You know what I'm talking about. Friends my ass. The conversations you and her are having is way more than friendship."

I knew then Chaun had been going through my phone again. I was getting to the point where the violations of privacy were becoming too frequent and was causing me to trust Chaun less and less.

"You have one more time to go through my phone and it's going to be a problem. You always want to know everything but you can't handle anything. Get out of here with that. You get your attitude together and start treating everyone involved with respect. I'm done with this." I snapped and walked out of the room.

The attitude and the atmosphere became more and more tense. Mia made the decision to leave and that was the end of the three of us. After the fallout and the communication ceased between Mia and Chaun, I continued seeing Mia. We began to become more vulnerable to one another and our emotions grew. Mia shared with me she had fallen in love with me and wanted more than anything something she could not have. She expressed how she wanted marriage, children, and the ability to be open about who she was in a relationship with. None of these things she could have with me because I was married. She never imagined herself falling in love with someone that was married and having to live the life as a mistress, but here she was.

Mia was not alone in her sentiments. I had fallen in love with her as well. When that happened, I had to accept the agonizing truth that I had fallen out of love with Chaun. After having pleaded with her and not having my needs met in our marriage for years I had withdrew and pulled away emotionally. I just had not realized how serious the disconnect had become until my love for Mia had blossomed.

The attraction between Mia and I became increasingly more intense and we could not stop. Even the few times we tried; we were drawn back to one another like a magnet to steel. But as we continued the affair became toxic. The entanglement of emotions became the source of tension which erupted into arguments and fights. It was a situation where we were blowing up at each other but it truly was never about what it appeared to be on the surface. It really stemmed from Mia wanting more from me and I not being able to give it to her. But she deserved what she was asking for.

She was an outstanding woman and if I was single there would be no question that I would have committed to her.

It eventually became too much and Mia made the choice to walk away. Ultimately, she chose herself. She could no longer sacrifice what she wanted to appease me. She knew that the marriage Chaun and I shared was strained but she refused to be another reason for the deterioration. Whatever my decision was about Chaun and I she wanted me to be able to make that without her being an influence.

Her choice to walk away from me hurt me to my core. I had fallen in love with Mia and could no longer see my life without her in it. I had become attached to her and my heart was now invested in her. An emotional affair is the riskiest thing that a relationship can endure and very few can recover from the extent of damage that it can cause. Once you attach yourself to someone emotionally and that person is ripped away from you, the pain that is felt runs deep. I was left confused, hurt, angry, and disappointed. I was left with my wife who I still loved but had failed to respond to my needs and betrayed me. And now I had lost the woman that I had fallen in love with and could now see in my future. How was I supposed to go on from here?

"Karma can manifest in varying forms. It was finally time for me to face my own...REJECTION."

- Candy

CHAPTER

Ten

Life After an Affair

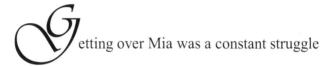etting over Mia was a constant struggle for me. I had gone into the situation with her and Nya only seeking my physical needs be met and ended up finding so much more. Everyone references karma to explain away certain circumstances they find themselves in or rationalize why they are experiencing the things they are enduring. If karma is as it is defined then it can come in various forms. Just because you lie does not mean your karma will be someone lying to you. Or if you cheat, does not mean your karma will be someone cheating on you. What I will say is in my

relationship with Tamia, karma came back and did a number on me. I ended up finding my heart entangled with a woman that was not mine. I ended up being hurt in the end and spending a lot of time trying to heal and move beyond the point all while still having Chaun in the forefront trying to work things out with me.

After Mia and I terminated all communication with one another that was when the work truly began for me. When you are trying to move past a situation you must be willing to be honest with yourself about things you may have tried to ignore or run from. The biggest thing I had to admit to myself and truly accept was the fact that I loved two women. There were days where I missed Mia to the point where I was hardly even present even though I was sitting right there with Chaun. My body was still in the home we shared but my mind and a major part of my heart was with Mia.

Despite my conflicted feelings, I decided to try to make things work with Chaun. Our relationship was in a very fragile state and I knew it was going to take a tremendous amount of effort on my part to refocus and give Chaun my undivided attention again. After having moved from one affair to the next, falling in love with another woman, that relationship ending, and now trying to mend my marriage we were thrust into yet another trying time.

Chaun was preparing for a major surgery. Even though we had had our challenges and our marriage was strained I had vowed to be there for her through sickness and in health and for better or worse. After all, she was still my best friend and I would do anything and everything for her. I knew she would need me more than ever after this surgery and I was going to help her through her recovery and take care of her wholeheartedly.

In the weeks leading up to her surgery I solicited the help of my family in order to help me with KenKay so I could be there every moment with Chaun. My mother and aunt had agreed to take care of the twins so I could be there during her surgery and stay overnight in the hospital. My grandmother chose to cook food for us since Chaun was going to be unable to for a few weeks. My Godmother decided to be with me at the hospital so I would not have to be alone. Chaun's mother planned to come and stay a few days when Chaun was released from the hospital to assist in caring for her while I took care of the kids. It was a huge effort that had to be orchestrated by many, but we wanted to make this work to make it as stress free as possible for Chaun.

"Are you ready for tomorrow?" I asked Chaun as we packed our bag for the hospital.

"I am. I'm a little nervous because I have never had surgery or even had to stay in the hospital before.

The last time I stayed in the hospital, we were having KenKay." she answered.

"True. But you know I will be there with you the entire time."

"I know baby. I appreciate you for everything."

The next day came and all players were in place to make everything happen. Chaun had to drive herself to the hospital so I could drop the twins off at school. Arrangements were made for my mom to pick them up after. My Godmother was ready to head to the hospital with me after the kids were in daycare. I made it just as they were beginning to prep Chaun for surgery. The doctor came into the room and talked to us followed by the anesthesiologist. Everything went quickly and before I knew it, they were ready to wheel her away.

"It's time. I love you and I'll see you when you come out." I said as I kissed Chaun sweetly on her forehead.

"I love you more."

"Mrs. Johnson, you have to leave your phone behind." the nurse said to Chaun spotting her phone sitting on the bed next to her leg.

"Here babe." Chaun said as she handed me her phone.

The nurse continued and then they were gone. I sat there for a moment with Chaun's phone in my hand and a level of anxiousness came over me that was so strong that I almost became nauseous. It had been years since I felt this feeling but I remembered the last time I felt it I discovered something that changed my life. As I sat there talking with my Godmother the feeling would not let me go. I had an internal struggle with myself knowing I had become furious with Chaun when she went through my phone but now, I was wanting to do the same thing. I felt this was the opportunity I finally had to determine whether the feelings I had been having for years were true about Chaun being unfaithful. You can usually always confirm if someone is cheating through their call log, text messages, or emails and here I was with access to all of it.

I was going to do it. I tapped the button on the side of the phone and the screen lit up. There was a screensaver of Chaun and I on the lock screen and it almost made me feel bad. After a short pause I swiped the screen and to my surprise there was no lock code. Chaun had removed the lock code she had on her phone that she claimed was to keep the kids from being able to get into her phone. I had always felt it was more so I could not get into her phone during the rare occasions she did not have the phone with her.

I dived into the phone and read message after message, checked her contacts, looked through her email, and watched a few video messages back and forth between her and some friends. At first glance, it seemed like I was wrong and Chaun had not been unfaithful. Yet, the feeling would not alleviate so I continued looking.

"What are you doing? You are really focused on something in your phone. Everything ok?" My Godmother said when she realized my attention was divided from the conversation.

"I am not sure yet." I responded.

"What do you mean?" she quizzed.

"I have to be honest. This isn't my phone. This is Chaun's phone." I admitted.

"Candy! What are you doing?"

"I told you I always thought Chaun was or had cheated. So now I get a chance to really see."

"Are you prepared for what you might find?" she asked.

"Yes. I need to know so I can be able to move on. I have felt this way for too long and if I am going to really try to make our marriage work, I need to know." I answered.

I continued looking for a little while longer and then it happened. I came across a provocative picture that I knew I had never received from Chaun. So, the question then became, if she had not sent the picture to me, then who had she sent it to? It appeared to me that she had done a fairly good job covering her tracks but this one little nugget was all I needed to confirm the women's intuition I had experienced for years. I sat there hurt, angry, and disappointed. I shared with my Godmother what I had found. She tried to explain it away because she truly loved Chaun and thought she was the best thing for me. But I knew better. I knew she had lied to me about other things in the past and this was just confirmation of what I already knew. Before closing the phone, I sent myself the picture so I could ensure I had it in case she attempted to go in and delete it later.

I had so many questions and I wanted to address this as soon as Chaun was conscious again but I knew this was not the right time. As angry and hurt as I was, I still loved her and I wanted to take care of her during her recovery. I swallowed everything I was feeling and tucked it away. When she came out of surgery I waited until she was admitted into her room for the night and I continued with everything as planned. I rushed home to our babies to feed them and bathe them for my mom to stay with them for the night. I made sure I had everything I needed and returned to the hospital to stay the night. I continued to love and support her despite my overwhelming desire to just leave her there in the hospital and go home to be with our babies. I fought with myself as I made sure she ate, insured she was warm, rubbed her feet, and cared for her the entire time she was recovering.

It was suffocating to have to deal with so many emotions and not be able to act on or express majority of them. Love is many things but one thing it will never be is selfish. This was not about me right now. It was about my wife having a major surgery and having weeks of recovery ahead of her. I had to continue to love and support her past my own personal feelings of betrayal. It was not an easy feat by far but it had to be done.

A few days after Chaun's surgery she was cleared to go home. I packed all our things into our bag and assisted her into the wheelchair so the transporter could take her down to the exit of the hospital.

"Are you ok?" I asked her as we walked down the sterile hallway of the hospital.

"Yes. I have some pain but it's not that bad." she replied.

"What's your pain on a scale of one to ten?" I asked. I always gauged her pain on a scale because I knew she had a high pain tolerance and depending on her response I could tell how serious it was and if I needed to act.

"It's about a five."

"Ok. I'll get you home and get you to bed so you can get comfortable. I got your prescriptions already. The twins will be so excited to see you but I will make sure they don't jump on you."

"Awww. I miss my babies." she said.

I carefully made the drive home making every effort to avoid any bumps that could aggravate Chaun's pain. As I made the drive, I kept playing things in my head repeatedly trying to determine when her infidelities could have taken place. I often prayed that my intuition was wrong because I was so deeply in love with her but another part of me knew my intuition had never been wrong. My heart ached and my anger grew but I saved face and continued with what I planned to do for Chaun.

We made it home without incident and I got Chaun in the house, up the stairs, and settled in our bed. I fed her and gave her pain medicine so she could rest. The next day Chaun's mom came as planned to assist me with her. She stayed with us for three days. During her stay, it was becoming progressively harder for me to keep the secret that I was holding. On the second day my mother-in-law was there we were able to get Chaun downstairs so she could rest in the leather couch recliner and move around. Chaun's mom went upstairs and it finally came to a head.

"I just want you to know that I know what you did. I know you've been cheating and I would appreciate it if you would be a woman and admit it." I said curtly to Chaun.

"Baby what are you talking about?" she responded.

"You know what I am talking about. Question is, are you finally willing to admit it?"

"I don't know what you are talking about. I don't know how many times I have to tell you that I love you and I have never cheated on you." Chaun said.

"So that is your choice?" I asked.

"What do you mean?"

I stared at her and heard Chaun's mom returning from upstairs. "You are making the choice to continue to lie so just know that I know and things are going to change drastically because of it."

Just as I finished my statement Chaun's mom reappeared and the conversation ceased. Chaun looked as if she had seen a ghost and I knew in that moment it was the beginning of the end. There was no way I was going to be able to move past this not knowing the truth. The things that I despise the most are liars and lack of loyalty and she had just presented both of those things to me.

Over the next couple of weeks, I continued to ask and urge Chaun to tell me the truth. She continued to try to minimize the information I had found in her phone. Yet, each time I pushed the envelope she would give a little more than she had given before. I came up with the idea of telling her someone had already informed me of the details of her infidelities to see if that would get her to talk. The truth of the matter was, no one had told me anything. Eventually, Chaun finally confessed.

As I laid in our bedroom alone watching TV the email notification sounded on my phone. Chaun was in the guest room because I no longer wanted to share a bed with her. I picked up my phone and it was an email from Chaun. I stared at the subject of the unread email, "The Truth". I contemplated for a moment whether I was truly ready to receive what I had been asking for. I also wondered if this was going to be the actual truth or just more bits and pieces being fed to me to win me back.

I opened the email and began to read it. As I processed the words that had been sent to me electronically from the other room, I could not believe everything that was being laid out. To my dismay there had been numerous women that spanned over three years. She admitted to cheating on me with one of my clients, meeting girls on a dating site, and even crossed the line with her friend's girlfriend. In reading this I came to the realization that majority of my marriage had been a complete lie. Then I read the email again and became sick to my stomach. In reviewing the timeline, I realized that this had been going on when I was enduring the grueling pregnancy with KenKay.

Who was this woman I was married to? The woman I was madly in love with had betrayed me beyond repair. My heart broke all over again. In the email she expressed that she felt she owed me the truth since I had made the decision that I no longer wanted the marriage. I could not help but to think this was not the whole truth. She informed me that despite the exchanging of nude pictures, the inappropriate conversations, and the secret meetings between her and my client that she had not had a sexual relationship with anyone. That was the hardest thing for me to believe. How could a person exchange pictures and talk sexually but never act on it?

We exchanged emails back and forth for a little while and I expressed how hurt and angry I was. I let her know that I did not believe this was it and that I still felt she was not being completely honest with all she had done. I did not think she really had incentive to give me the full truth now anyway since I had already made the decision to leave the relationship.

This email was only the beginning because I had so many questions, I had to get the answers to and I wanted details. I had to take the night to ingest what I had been given so far. One thing I was usually good at doing was dissecting information and finding holes in the story and what I was provided so far had a lot of holes in it.

"Do you really believe that she has given me the full truth?" I asked Wisdom a few days later. I had to talk to someone about all of this. I felt like I had been living my days in a fog lately.

"Not based on everything you have shared. I can definitely understand why you feel the way you do" Wisdom responded.

"So what choice does that leave me with?" I asked.

"I can't tell you what you should do but all I know is that once the trust is broken then there is usually no recovering from that." she said.

"You said a mouthful there."

"It is sad that she is losing everything and is still unwilling to give you what you need to heal and move on." she said.

"Exactly. It is like a constant slap in my face and makes me question if she really loved me at all."

I went to Chaun and asked her to provide details on her extramarital affairs. She claimed none of it was sexual but now it was time for her to really own the things she had done.

"So, I've read and re-read your email. From what you have shared this was going on during my pregnancy." I said.

"No, it didn't. I would never have done anything like that during your pregnancy. I was too busy taking care of you." Chaun retorted.

"Ok. Tell me what did happen then." I probed.

"What all do you want to know?" she asked sheepishly.

"Everything." I barked.

As we talked, Chaun slowly recounted details of the deceptive acts she had performed. Learning the details were a lot and spanned over several conversations because as the information was shared my anger would flare up and I would have to walk away for the night and sometimes days after. During this first session I learned that she had exchanged phone numbers with a client from my office. She advised that it started innocently but then the girl learned that Chaun was a lesbian and she began to flirt with her. Chaun did inform her that she was married to me but the flirtations continued. Chaun then began to reciprocate the flirtations. I asked her when this began and she lied initially. I think she knew the devastation it would cause if I discovered this happened during my pregnancy.

Yet, one of the things about gathering details about the situation is eventually the person is going to be forced to tell the truth either by voluntarily giving it or the lies that have been told will not add up and the truth will come out involuntarily. So, as she informed me that she had met with her secretly on several occasions on her way home from the office that was the nugget that I needed. This was how I was able to prove this happened during my pregnancy. This was easy to determine because prior to my pregnancy we moved in tandem. When I was in the office, so was Chaun. When I was not in the office it was because we were together. The only times she would have been able to move without me was when I was too sick to go to the office. After persisting and backing her into a corner, she finally admitted it was going on during that time.

I was furious. To think back on how difficult my pregnancy was and knowing she was doing these things was terrible. I remembered there being times I would be at home waiting for her to return from the office during the day barely eating because I was too afraid to eat knowing I would be sick after. I would wait for her to return home because I knew she would be able to help me eat and be there when I got sick. Knowing she was lying and cheating on me during this time diminished the fact that she cared for me and cleaned up after me when I was sick. It made me wonder if she did those things for me out of obligation, out of guilt, or out of love. I was second guessing everything at this point.

After digesting the betrayal from my pregnancy, I still wanted and needed to know more. I went to

Chaun again dissecting the email. During the times I was begging for her attention and pleading for us to reconnect she was distracted by the other women she was entertaining. It was making more and more sense now and I wondered why she even stayed. If she was so unhappy with me why did she string me along and continue to sell me a lie of a marriage. I wanted to know more about the additional women. She informed me of the social networking and dating app she had signed up on. Chaun claimed it was a source of entertainment for her. For her it was a means to seek the validation she wanted that I had stopped giving her when my business opened. I had to admit that I did stop showing her as much affection, giving her compliments, and adoring her as I once had. But the stress of the business and me being so determined to be successful so I could provide for us took precedence.

She informed me she would talk to various women and flirt with some that she found attractive or who found her attractive. All the women were in other states and she said she never met any of them in person. For me that translated to her just not having the opportunity to foster any sexual relationships with these women.

This had me continuously second guessing myself. In the past she had finally admitted to me after years of our intimacy fading that it was due to her feeling of disrespect with the way I treated her in my business and that I had gained weight. I had already had to try to overcome the teardown of my confidence because I felt as if my wife was no longer physically attracted to me but now I was thrust into the thought of whether or not that was a lie and it was really because she was seeing other women. I felt like I was being mentally toyed with and could not make sense of it all. The mountain of lies and deception continued to grow and the idea of being able to move forward in this marriage filled with lies, deception, disrespect, and disloyalty continued to become increasingly difficult for me.

Continuing to put the timelines together made me realize that Chaun's indiscretions started years before I ever had my first affair. Learning that she had been unfaithful to me long before I ever dishonored our vows infuriated me even more. The fact that she played the victim and besmudged my character to some of our close friends and family when my affairs surfaced was yet another notch added to the tally of betrayals that were mounting. With the knowledge now that Chaun had been the catalyst that catapulted us into this dark hole that was leading our marriage into ruin was a lot to bear.

The next few weeks were very emotional as I continued to process all Chaun had done. I had to sort through my feelings. Even though I was so hurt and angry I still loved this woman. She was my everything at one point. The pedestal that I once placed Chaun on however, had crumbled into a million pieces. I was left with the memory of who I thought she was and had to deal with the truth of the immense betrayal I was faced with.

As I sat in my truck in the parking lot of the courthouse, I was faced with the magnitude of the decision I was making. I took a few deep breaths and made my way inside the building. After walking through the metal detectors, I went to the bank of elevators and pressed the up arrow. My hands began to shake a little and my palms got sweaty as the doors to the elevator opened. I stepped inside and pushed the number three. When the elevator reached the requested floor, I hesitated for a moment before getting off. I stood there for a few moments watching the various people coming and going. I wondered how many of these other people were here making the same life altering decision I was making. Was there anyone else here dealing with hurt and pain from an unfaithful spouse?

I made my way to the wall of forms and went through them all. I gathered the forms I needed and returned to my truck. I sat there again and tears began to fall from my eyes. When I proposed to Chaun six years ago I thought we would be forever. I never signed up for any of the things that had happened over the last three years. I sat there trying to figure out where it all went wrong. What was the turning point that sent us down this downward spiral? What more could I have done to insure something like this never happened? My tears shifted from sadness to anger and I knew this was the right decision. I wiped the tears away and made the drive back home.

I pulled into the garage and walked into the house. KenKay were upstairs in their rooms playing and Chaun was downstairs in the kitchen preparing dinner.

"Hey." she said as I entered the kitchen.

"Hey." I responded.

I walked over to Chaun and gave her a hug. I held her tight for a moment and she grabbed me back. I let her go and handed her the papers I was holding onto in my hand.

I handed the papers to her and said, "I want a divorce. When you are ready, we can sit down and fill everything out."

She stared at me and tears started to fall. I walked out of the kitchen and headed upstairs. This was the end.

"To seek is to suffer. The truth is the light in darkness. Knowing the truth requires action and accountability."

- Candy

CHAPTER

Eleven

Love and Trust

Making the decision to end my marriage was devastating. No one goes into a marriage thinking it is going to end. When I planned that elaborate proposal, I was truly planning for my forever and my happily ever after. But now I was left with the feeling that I had made a fool of myself and made the biggest mistake of my life. I loved and trusted Chaun more than I had ever anyone else from my past. It was even a deeper disappointment thinking back to all the sacrifices I had made with my family and how reluctant I was to let my guard down after the betrayals from my past. I never thought Chaun would have the ability to be so dishonest and disloyal to me.

Prior to giving Chaun the divorce papers I truly believe she thought this would pass and I would be able to move on with the relationship with time like we had in the past. But this time was different. I could not recover from this. I had faith in Chaun that she was the one and I had made the right decision, but I was wrong. The tricky thing about trust is that it is a gamble. When you trust someone, you are believing and hoping they will not break that trust. Unfortunately, this gamble had ended badly for me.

A few days after I had given Chaun the divorce papers we finally sat down at the kitchen table after putting the twins to bed so we could complete the paperwork.

"You really don't care." I said to Chaun as she pulled her seat up to the table with her pen in hand.

"What do you mean?" she asked.

"You seem like this is nothing for you."

Chaun looked up at me with tears welling up in her eyes. "Candy this is the hardest thing I have ever had to do. But this is what you want. I did not ask you for a divorce."

"You didn't give me a choice. Look at all the lies you told...everything you did to me."

"Candy, I was not alone in the betrayal." she blurted out.

"Yeah but I owned what I did. You acted like a victim and drug my name through the mud telling everyone how horrible I was when all along you were doing the same thing!" I hissed.

"I was not doing the same thing. I wasn't sleeping with anyone."

"That's what your mouth says. And the fact that you can sit here and continue to lie to me is the exact reason we are sitting here filling out these papers. This is how I know I made the right decision." I exclaimed.

"What do you want me to do? Do you want me to make up some story admitting that I had sex with someone when I really did not? I told you the truth." Chaun said.

"Only because you felt like you had no other choice. You were backed into a corner. You would not have admitted anything had I not went through your phone or kept coming at you with it. Save the lies for one of the many hoes you were fucking." I snapped.

I was furious and did not want to talk anymore. We sat in silence and filled out the petition for divorce. We agreed on a visitation schedule for the kids, who would be able to claim them or their taxes, financial support for daycare and other expenses, and declined any form of spousal support. We were doing this without attorneys and knew this would be the easiest most efficient way to get it done quickly. I wanted out as soon as possible so I could move on with my life. After we finished the forms I retired to our bedroom and Chaun went to the guest room as we had done for the last few weeks.

The following day we took KenKay to daycare and made our way back to the courthouse. We made the drive to the courthouse in silence and Chaun stared out the window. I was so angry that she had put us in this situation. It was because of her that I would now be a single mother. I had a plan for my life which is why I waited until I was married to have children. She had ruined that for me. We made our way to the third floor and stood in line waiting our turn to submit our paperwork and pay the necessary fees. The clerk who assisted us was nice but handled everything like it was just a routine transaction. But for us this was much more than a simple transaction. This was the end of our family, the end of a union, the separation of two lives that had been fused together for almost eleven years. But for the clerk she reviewed each form to make sure it was complete, stamped the necessary forms, checked the judge's schedule to assign us a date, and gave us a receipt for the fees paid. After giving us our copies and explaining the next steps, the transaction was simply ended with, "Can I help the next person please!" and we stepped away from the counter.

When we got out to the hallway to get back on the elevator, I could see that Chaun was crying again.

"Are you ok?" I asked

I still hated to see her cry. I still wanted to be the one to dry her tears and take her pain away. But that was no longer my role.

"I'm fine." she whispered.

Over the next several weeks we carried on as amicably as we could. We continued to care for the twins and made sure we conducted ourselves as normal as possible in front of them. One of the biggest things we wanted to do was to make sure this did not affect them negatively. Our court date was set for February 4th and as the day grew near my anger slowly began to transition to sadness. We made the decision for Chaun to move out by the end of April so she could have time to find a place to stay and for us to make all the necessary changes we needed to make with the household affairs.

There were moments when I second guessed my decision. Yet, during those moments of weakness I would look at the photo evidence I had and the email "The Truth" and knew I had to move forward as planned. The weeks eventually went by and it was the day for us to go before the judge to determine if our petition for divorce would be granted. Chaun met me at the courthouse and we sat in silence, like strangers, in the hallway until it was time to enter. We entered the courtroom along with several other couples who were all there in various stages of their divorce proceedings. Some of them accompanied by lawyers. There were even some lawyers there who were acting solely on behalf of their clients.

Chaun and I sat and watched as case after case was called forward. One thing we noticed was that the judge was anything but nice to those who were coming before him.

"I hope this goes well. You know I do not have the best temper." I whispered to Chaun.

She smiled a little bit knowing that I was a bit of a hot head. "If it becomes too much just let me do the talking. I do not have enough money with me right now to have to bail you out of jail."

I giggled a little and realized at the end of the day, she was still a close friend. I wondered if one day we could get back to the friendship we once had years ago before we decided to cross the line into dating. I knew I would have a lot of healing and forgiveness to endure but I was willing to do it. As I was getting lost in my thoughts I was shaken back to the present when I heard the judge call our case.

We approached the bench with all our paperwork in hand. The judge went through a series of questions and verified all the information that we provided. He was less than kind and we wondered if it was because we were black, a same-sex couple, or a combination of the two. Whatever the reason was, we could not wait until this moment was over. It was clear he had some form of personal feelings that prohibited him for being kind during this very sensitive and fragile moment for us and several other couples in the courtroom.

After about thirty minutes of discussing our irreconcilable differences, visitation schedule for KenKay, discussing how property would be divided, and any financial responsibility, the judge signed off on everything and our divorce was final. This woman I had given myself to almost six years before was no longer my wife. We walked out of the courtroom and went our separate ways. We had several hours before the twins had to be picked up from school and I just needed time to decompress. I was dealing with a lot of emotions and honestly felt a little lost. The world I had come to know over the last eleven years was being stripped away and I was forced to accept the realization that I was now going to have to establish a completely new world.

I got into my truck and made a call to Wisdom. I needed someone to talk to.

"It's over." I said when she answered the phone.

"How do you feel?" she asked.

"Honestly, I don't know. Am I supposed to be happy, sad, or mad? I think I am confused right now." I replied.

"That's understandable. You are probably going to feel that way for a little while. You have to have time to process everything. There will be some good days and bad days too as things continue to change."

Wisdom tried her hardest to comfort me and allowed me to vent. I do not even think if half of the things I was saying really made sense. But as I drove, I talked. Eventually I felt a sense of calm come over me and I was ready to head home.

The next couple of months before Chaun moved out were difficult to say the least. There were moments when it seemed like we could barely be in the same room with one another. Then there were other moments where I felt like I was getting my friend back. The emotional stresses were a lot and I looked forward to the moment when things would level out and we could settle into our new normal.

It is funny though because after Chaun left and it was just me and KenKay I had more time to think and process all that had happened. I would wonder if I overreacted, had we done all we could to try to overcome all the damage that had been done, or was this really the right decision. Everything in the house reminded me of Chaun and then I had to accept another hard truth…I still loved her. Yet, at the same time, I was still hurt and angry.

Chaun continued to visit so she could spend time with the twins. If I needed her to pick them up from school or be with them when I had other obligations to tend to, she was always there. She never skipped a beat. That was one quality she possessed that I could never take from her. She was an amazing parent to the kids and I could not have handpicked a better person to be the second mommy to our babies. It was one of the things that I always adored about her.

As the weeks continued, we started spending progressively more time with one another as a family. There is a cliché that says, "absence makes the heart grow fonder" and I wondered if that was what was happening for us. The nights when she was not there, I found myself thinking about her and wondering what she was doing. When she would call to talk to KenKay I always made time to spend a little time on the phone with her as well. Conversely, I think it was the same for her. There would be times when she would randomly text me just to say hello or ask me what I had to eat that day. It was obvious that we still cared for one another.

"I miss her." I said to Wisdom.

"I would be surprised if you didn't. She was your wife and you guys were together for eleven years. You practically raised each other." she replied.

"I guess you're right. We sorta did. We accomplished so much together. But look at all the damage and pain we caused each other." I said.

"Yeah. You two went through some storms and trenches. But what couple doesn't?" she asked.

"But can a relationship rebound from this level of pain?" I asked. I was talking to Wisdom but I think I was more so talking to myself.

"I think it can but it will take an immense amount of work." Wisdom answered as I was lost in my own thoughts.

"Sometimes one of the biggest questions you have to ask yourself when it comes to contemplating continuing or returning to a relationship is if you are better with that person or without them. Think about the last couple of months you have been without Chaun. Has things been easier for you mentally and emotionally. Or have you been in a state of confusion or loss?" she continued.

"Confusion or loss?" I inquired. I was not quite sure what she meant by that.

"Yes. Have you heard someone say they are lost without someone? Like nothing feels the same. You don't have the same joy you once had with things. You know...lost." she explained.

That explanation made me pause. I do not think I had really given it much thought. I was so busy trying to let go and get used to life without Chaun that I never took the time to reflect on her absence.

"You have given me something to think about."

Wisdom looked at me and smiled. "When you take the time to evaluate those things and truly accept it, you will know what your answer is."

That conversation with Wisdom was like being given a homework assignment. I went home and after getting the kids to bed I showered and climbed into bed. I took several deep breaths to settle my mind so I could do what Wisdom said I should. I thought back on the last couple of months Chaun was gone and I realized that nothing seemed the same anymore. I felt lonely without her. Even doing the things I did on an everyday basis seemed empty. Laying there in our king-sized bed I reached over to her side of the bed and the realization hit me like a ton of bricks. I wanted Chaun home.

"Some marriages end when people stop loving each other. But ours ended when we stopped hurting each other."

- Candy

CHAPTER

Twelve

Reclaiming Love

After coming to the realization that I wanted

Chaun back I had to figure out what that would look
like. How do you go from divorcing someone to
wanting to be with them again? I knew Chaun still
loved me so I was not too worried about her not
being willing to reconcile. I just really wanted to
make sure this was the right decision for the both of
us. Chaun had started spending increasingly more
time at the house and I was happy when she did. I
thought I was ready for her to move back home
after she had begun to stay overnight at times.

Chaun had just finished doing a live video on Facebook. It was a fairly new feature that we had begun to see people use. It was sparked from a really good conversation we were having in response to a clip of an episode of Braxton Family Values we had seen. In the clip they were talking about whether you should address a cheating partner if you were not willing to do anything about it.

"Ok. Well, I am going to head home." Chaun said grabbing her purse.

I walked over to Chaun and grabbed her purse from her hand.

"You don't have to leave." I said.

"I didn't bring any clothes with me." she retorted.

"That's ok. I think you left a few things here the last time. And you can always wash if you need to." I said.

"Ok. You sure?" she asked.

"Yes. Truth is, I don't want you to have to leave again." I said.

"What do you mean?"

"I love you. I never stopped loving you. I want you to come home and let's see where this goes." I replied.

"I love you too. I would love to come back." Chaun said with a smile on her face.

"I know it's going to take work on both ends but I am willing to do the work with you." I pulled Chaun close and hugged her.

Over the next few days, Chaun moved back into the house. I was happy to have her back. She was still like the yin to my yang and as soon as she returned it was like everything went back to normal. We moved like a well-oiled machine and during the time she was gone that machine was out of whack. During Chaun's transition back to the house, we received a huge response to the video Chaun had done. So many people wanted us to do more videos addressing more topics to get our feedback.

We thought about what we could do a second video about and reflected on all we had been through. When you go through trials and tribulations, there are times when you think you are the only one experiencing that level of pain. Yet, that could be the furthest from the truth. There are so many others going through the same or very similar circumstances. So, we decided on a second video topic and I agreed to be in the video with Chaun this time. Again, this video was met with positive feedback.

As a result of some of our friends and family members requesting more videos from us, we decided to make a separate page called, Candy &

Chaun. After the first few videos we realized that it was really kind of therapeutic and it gave us another way to connect with one another. At the time we had no idea it would grow to be something that thousands of people would enjoy. But it became another tie that bound us and as more people began to watch our videos, we quickly learned that we were also helping other people at the same time.

As we continued to create content it assisted us in being able to have some of the difficult conversations that we may have otherwise avoided about what we had been through with the infidelity in our marriage. There would be times when we would wrap up our video and then continue to talk for hours afterward. It gave us the opportunity to sort through feelings and emotions that we knew were still there and needed to be addressed if we were going to move forward with the reconciliation. We were still in a space of uncertainty because I had never tried to reconcile with anyone who I considered as an ex before. Normally when I was done with a relationship I was completely done.

I had been giving so much thought to reclaiming our love and rededicating myself to Chaun. Through it all I never stopped loving her and knew I wanted to spend the rest of my life with her. There was a very important date that was approaching and neither of us really knew how to address it or handle it. That date was July 16th and it would have been our six-year wedding anniversary. Yet, since we had just gotten our divorce five months ago, we wondered how it would feel and whether we should acknowledge it or not.

I knew that if we were going to really give our relationship another chance it was going to be a lot of work on both sides. We were going to have to go to counseling so we could navigate through all the muddy waters and truly heal so our past would not continue to contaminate our present and future. The worst thing you can do is try to ignore something and think that it will go away because it never does. I finally made the firm decision that Chaun was who I wanted and I was ready to commit myself to her again.

I thought about how I could make it special and ensure that she would be able to recognize how serious I was about my decision. I decided to utilize the growing platform we had as a way for me to publicly profess my love for her. I also wanted to publicly apologize for the things I had done privately to devastate her.

It was July 15th and I had been trying to get everything together for the surprise I wanted to do for Chaun that night. I told her that I thought we should take a break from Candy & Chaun that night and not do a video. I used the excuse that maybe we should just relax and spend some time watching TV. I had also disappeared a couple of times during the day leaving the house to gather different things I would need for the surprise. I knew Chaun was probably wondering what in the world was going on and why I was acting so strange that day, but I was working hard to make this something that she would not forget.

The moment had arrived and I was ready to execute what I believed would demonstrate how serious I was about taking this step with her again. We were in our bedroom watching TV.

"Babe I'll be right back. I'm about to go get a snack. You want something?" I asked Chaun as I got up from my chair.

"No, I'm ok." she replied.

I hurried out of the room and knew I had a limited amount of time before she would come looking for me. I had discreetly snuck Chaun's phone out of the room with me because I needed that as a part of what I was planning to do. Earlier in the day I had strategically placed everything I needed in a place where I could get to it quickly and get everything staged. I raced up and down the stairs as quietly as I could making sure everything was as I needed it to be. I checked myself in the mirror and then set up our phones in the guest room which we had coined "The Honeycomb Hideout" for our videos.

I sat there for a few seconds nervous. My heart was pounding and my hands were sweaty. I had never done anything like this before and I hoped it went as planned. I pushed the buttons to go live on both phones and the video started. I explained to everyone watching that I needed their help in letting Chaun know that I wanted to give us another try. I wanted us to commit to one another again and go to counseling to help us mend our relationship. After spending a few minutes letting everyone know what the purpose of the video was it was time for me to go get Chaun. I went to our bedroom holding a blindfold.

"Chaun I have a little surprise for you." I said as I peeked in the bedroom door.

"What is it? You know I like surprises." Chaun said like a little kid.

"You have to come with me. But first, I have to put this blindfold on you."

Chaun looked at me with a look of curiosity. But she complied and turned around so I could slip the red blindfold over her eyes. I gently tied it around the back of her head and lead her out the bedroom.

"Don't you let me run into a wall or fall down the stairs." she said as she clumsily followed my lead.

"Don't you always say you trust me? Then trust me now." I replied.

I led Chaun into the black and white guest room where the videos were still rolling on our phones. I sat her down on the seat in front of the cameras and sat down next to her. I removed the blindfold and I began to speak the words I had practiced repeatedly in my head. I hoped I would be able to get them out as easily as I had rehearsed despite my nervousness.

"I have to tell you something." I started.

"Ok." Chaun said hesitantly

"The reason that I'm live and the reason why I've been acting a little weird today is because I've been trying to surprise you. I wanted to talk to you and let you know how sorry I am for everything that we've been through. I hurt you. I disappointed you. I let you down. I broke your heart. I apologize for not only having an affair but I also apologize for not holding true to my vows to you. I want nothing more than to have another opportunity to be with you. I love you. I'm ready to do whatever it takes to fix our relationship. My suggestion is that we go to counseling and we take it one day at a time. I want to be exclusive to you. I want you to be exclusive to me. But most importantly, I want to show you tonight the ultimate act of submission."

"Wow. Wow. I am speechless." Chaun responded as tears started to fill her eyes.

I continued and asked for her forgiveness. I needed to know that she forgave me so that we could move forward and be able to really commit to the reconciliation and the work that was going to be ahead of us.

"I forgive you. But I told you before that I forgave you." Chaun said.

It was now time for me to show Chaun the remainder of the surprise I had for her. I asked her to grab the phones and to head out of the room. When she opened the door, she was greeted by red rose petals I had scattered in the hallway and down the stairs leading to the great room.

"Oh my goodness Candy. This is beautiful" Chaun gasped.

She made her way down the stairs and I had laid out a foot bath for her with a glass of champagne and a card to express my love for her. I instructed her to sit on the couch in front of the foot bath.

"Awww. There's rose petals in the water." she said as she pointed the camera to the water so the viewers could see on the phone she was holding.

I wanted to explain a little more to everyone watching as well.

"So, for those that haven't figured it out yet, my ultimate act of submission is to wash her feet."

After wrapping up the video I did just that. I kneeled in front of Chaun and I washed her feet. While washing her feet I wanted her to know how much I loved her and how much she meant to me. This was the first major step we took together in the hopes of repairing what we had both torn apart over the years. I had my reservations but I knew it was because of fear and succumbing to my vulnerability. I was having to rebuild the trust for the very woman that had destroyed it and she had to do the same. It was a difficult road for both of us but we promised one another we would try and give it one hundred percent. We knew there were going to be difficult days, hard discussions, and times when we may want to give up. Yet, we were ready to fight. We had been through so much, accomplished so much, and built a lot together and it was time to see what more we could do together.

A little over a month later we began counseling. The first therapist we found was not a good fit for us. We knew with us being a same sex couple we really wanted to make sure we found someone that was comfortable with our relationship and would treat us with the same level of respect as a heterosexual couple. The first therapist seemed like she was trying too hard to relate and be comfortable so we decided to find another one. The second one we found was excellent. She was attentive, fair, and extremely comfortable with our relationship. She truly gave the impression that she cared and helped Chaun and I hear each other at times when it was difficult to do so.

I had heard about people who went to counseling and how it can really open you up. A good therapist will make you address things you were either afraid to address or became too difficult to endure. And our therapist did just those things for us. There would be times when we would prepare for our sessions and be in a great mood but by the time the session was over, we barely wanted to speak to one another.

We really had to be willing to be vulnerable and transparent with one another in order to get the most out of our therapy sessions. During our first couple of sessions our therapist asked both of us what we wanted and how we felt. Chaun was sure she wanted the relationship and expressed that she was in love with me. I had to sit for a moment because I was not able to answer as confidently. I knew that I loved Chaun but I had to be honest. I was not all in and I had to make sure Chaun knew where I was on this journey.

"Candy, would you like to answer the question?" the therapist said after I had not answered after a few moments.

"I think I realize as we continue with our sessions that I have to admit some things. Chaun, you know how bad I was hurt by all that you did. We have been dealing with this for years and I realize that I am not in love with you anymore. I love you but it has been some time since I was in love with you. If I'm honest, I am probably one foot in and one foot out. But all I can say is that I will try and we can see what happens." I said.

Chaun looked at me and you could see the disappointment and sadness come over her.

"I understand. I know you are going to need time and I am willing to give you as much time as you need. I know this is something you have never done before." Chaun said softly.

We continued with our sessions and during one of them my world was rocked. I had been trying my hardest to move forward but I still did not think I knew the full truth with what Chaun had done. I still believed she had had a sexual relationship with other women even though she remained steadfast with the narrative that she had not. Then we were discussing her indiscretions and another detail that had never been shared surfaced while Chaun spoke.

"The relationship between me and Candy's client was wrong I know that. But it was never physical. I never really took her seriously because she joked a lot. She would even call KenKay her step kids knowing there was nothing going on between her and I. But that…."

"Stop. What did you just say?" I blurted out.

"What?" Chaun said as she was caught off guard when I cut her off.

"What did you say she called my kids?" I hissed.

"She joked and called them her step kids. But it was nothing like that." Chaun replied.

I was livid. How dare she sit here and say that another woman jokingly called my kids her step kids. That is not a joke. This further supported my feelings of Chaun not being honest. As we sat there, I literally had the feeling that I had made yet another mistake with trying to reconcile with her. The therapist tried to help us through this conversation for the remainder of the session but I was done. I did not want to talk anymore and I had shut down. I could no longer participate because my anger and disgust would not allow me.

After that session we talked more and Chaun tried to reassure me that it was never meant literally. She said the girl joked a lot and at times it was annoying to her. That meant nothing to me. For me, I felt she was again trying to minimize what she had done. I did not see anything humorous about some girl calling my kids her step kids. This was another hurdle we had to try to overcome. It caused friction between Chaun and I for a while. But we continued down the path we had started on. I had promised I would try so I continued. But I was getting to the point where if there was anything else to come out, I did not think I would be able to keep going on with this.

Over time we made it past that. We completed some additional therapy sessions and then made the decision to try to continue the journey on our own. We did gain a lot of helpful tools and strategies to use to help us navigate through the difficult times.

As time continued it seemed like things were getting better. We had even started talking about remarrying. We knew we did not want to have another wedding like before. We decided when we were ready it would be a destination wedding and those that could make it were welcome to come. But we never put any plans in motion because Chaun said she did not think we were ready yet. She kept emphasizing the fact that I was not in love with her and she knew it. But I got to the point where I wanted to convince her that I was in love with her. I even got her name tattooed on my arm along with the kid's names on a business trip to Las Vegas.

But in a way, I think I was trying to convince myself more than her. I felt like we were just moving along in a neutral state. It seemed as if we were progressing forward in a routine and my feelings were not progressing. I was waiting for the moment when I would fall back in love with Chaun but that moment never came. I was working to rebuild my trust in her and I did trust her with some things but I was unable to fully trust her again. It got to the point where I wondered if this was the culmination of our relationship. Had the relationship run its course? I did not want to spend the rest of my life in a lackluster relationship. I felt like there was so much more available.

There was a time when I felt butterflies around Chaun. I used to feel like my world was incomplete without her. Chaun used to be my beginning and end. But now, we felt more like friends than lovers to me. Then I started noticing that little things Chaun would do started bringing up old feelings and resentment. We started having disagreements that seemed like it was about one thing but it really was about so much more. I accepted the fact that as much as I thought I was getting past what Chaun had did, I had not. The damage was deeper than I thought and I really was not sure if I was going to be able to continue this.

The thing about deciding to reconcile with someone is that it does not mean it is set in stone or that it is going to be forever. I decided it was time for me to see what life was like without Chaun. We never gave ourselves the opportunity to truly heal. We divorced and then within four months we were right back together. It was finally time to rip the band aid off. I needed to experience life without her. If we were meant to be together, then I knew our paths would cross again. But for now, I was ready to finally separate. I just hoped Chaun would understand.

"Take the time to truly heal or you will never move forward. Life begins one step outside of your comfort zone."

- Candy

CHAPTER

Chirteen

The Final Goodbye

*T*here is something about the inevitable…it always comes. I had been trying to find the right time to talk to Chaun about my feelings and what our future held. But honestly, I do not think there is really a right time to tell someone you no longer want a relationship with them. I had attempted on a few different occasions but was not able to follow through. The funny thing about holding on to feelings and emotions they tend to bubble and boil over when you least expect it. It was literally like the cork exploding from a champagne bottle after the pressure has been released.

I had returned from a two-day business trip. Chaun had put the kids to bed and was waiting for me in the TV room. I had sat down to eat the food I picked up on the way home so I could eat before we did our Candy & Chaun video for the night. We started talking and somehow, we began to disagree on something. The small disagreement began to escalate and everything that I had suppressed and tried to ignore manifested itself in that moment.

"Candy, I do not know what else I can do. I am trying so hard to show you I'm not that person from before." Chaun exclaimed.

"Stop trying." I blurted out before I even knew what I was saying.

"What do you mean? Be sure on what you are saying." Chaun retorted.

"Just stop trying."

"Right now, or for good?" Chaun asked for clarification.

"For good. I can't do this anymore. I tried but this shows me that the small things keep turning into big things and it's because I can't get over what you did. I thought I had. I thought I could. But I can't. You caused too much damage and we can't keep going on like this."

"Are you sure?" Chaun asked.

"I'm sure."

"Ok. I respect your decision." Chaun said with tears streaming down her cheeks.

When I woke up that morning, I had no idea the day would end with the finale of my relationship. I really gave Chaun all my attention and I had tried for the last almost two years to regain any semblance of what we once had when our relationship was good. But I think we were holding on to what used to be and ignoring what it was and had become.

That night was an emotional night by far. Chaun cried unconsolably and there was nothing I could do. I had to stand firm in my decision and hoped that Chaun would understand once she was able to calm down and think about what I had explained to her. This decision had to be made. I could no longer love her the way I once did. The culmination of her actions damaged me to the point where I could no longer see her as the woman I once did. Prior to all of this I saw her as almost angelic. But now she not only reminded me of all the pain I had suffered in the past, she added additional layers of betrayal that were incomprehensible.

To be fair to both of us, it was time to let it go and see what life was like without one another. The Candy & Chaun video we were scheduled to do that night never happened. That weekend after the breakup was extremely difficult. I tried to be sensitive to Chaun as she processed everything but the tension was immense. What do you say to someone when it is evident that you had broken their heart? All I could do was give her the space she needed to process everything.

We eventually got to the point where we could talk again but the interactions were very mixed. One moment we would be laughing and joking, then the next moment Chaun was cold and reluctant to communicate. You could see the emotional rollercoaster we were both going through based on our hot and cold interactions with one another. It seemed to me that Chaun was taking the breakup harder than the divorce and I was curious to see if I was correct.

"Can I ask you a question?" I asked Chaun.

"Sure." she answered.

"Which one was harder for you? The divorce or the breakup?" I inquired.

"To be honest, the breakup was harder for me." she said.

"Why? It seems like the divorce would have been worse because that was the end of our marriage."

"True. But I thought back on it and I think I realized it was because after the divorce I fell in love with you. Or at least maybe I fell deeper in love with you. I honestly have never felt this way before about anyone. I don't even think I knew what being in love really meant. I thought I did but it wasn't until I completely fell that I realized it." she explained.

"So you haven't been in love with me this whole time?" I said with shock in my voice.

"I guess not. But I knew I loved you. I knew you meant the world to me and I knew I wanted to be with you for the rest of my life. I loved you deeply. But I don't think I ever let myself completely fall until after the divorce when I lost you." she said.

"Wow. That says a lot." I said.

It was difficult to know that Chaun realized she had not even fell in love with me until after the divorce. To know she accepted my proposal years before and was not ready for that step made me feel even more foolish. I literally felt like I had wasted thirteen years of my life and the only good things that came from it were KenKay. But even that angered me because I never signed up to be a single mother. I purposefully waited to have kids until after I was married because I wanted the probability of a broken home to be limited as much as possible. Yet, here I was.

We made the difficult decision that it was necessary to go public with our breakup with our Candy & Chaun platform. The response from everyone that had grown to enjoy our videos and commentary was nothing short of shock and disbelief. But one thing we had always prided ourselves on was being honest and transparent about who we were and the journey we were embarking on when we first started the platform.

The one thing about the breakup of a couple that everyone has grown to love seeing together is that once it ends it seems like everyone else is just as heartbroken as the parties in the relationship. Sometimes it seemed like it was worse for the bystanders. But then again, nobody knew the depth of what all had transpired, so for them it seemed like the end of something great. But we were the furthest thing from it.

We navigated through another seven weeks under the same roof before Chaun moved out. This was the final step that solidified the breakup. We were at least able to get to a point where we were able to continue the Candy & Chaun brand. It was something we both loved and invested so much of ourselves in. We felt like the Candy & Chaun platform was bigger than us and served a bigger purpose.

Once Chaun was gone, I started my journey to my new life. I had to restructure my day to day life since she was no longer a part of it. The well-oiled machine that we once had, I now had to rebuild it with just one operator instead of two. I also had to face the difficult questions from KenKay about why "Mema" was not there. My once long days became even longer now that I was responsible for everything. There were many nights that I would go to bed exhausted. Then as I lay in bed before I drift off to sleep, I had to deal with my feelings of anger and resentment towards Chaun. She had single handedly ruined the plan I had for our lives.

Yet, the reality was, I could not get lost in my emotions and feelings. I had to be strong for the twins, focus on my business, and continue to be involved with my family. Each week I had to travel out of state to my office to ensure everything was running as it should and attend various meetings. It was a tremendous amount of pressure but I had to keep my head up and persevere.

Because of everything that was occurring it was easy for me to become reclusive. Absorbing all the thoughts and opinions from the public and my family was exhausting. Having to deal with everyone making me feel like I was wrong or the villain in the situation was frustrating to the say the least. How could anyone fault me for finally choosing me and wanting to have happiness. It was appalling to think there were those that would have rather seen me in an unfulfilling relationship because it would be better for the kids, or we looked good together, or whatever other frivolous reason that could be thought of to validate why Chaun and I should still be together.

I withdrew socially, except for the Candy & Chaun videos we still managed to create. It was becoming normal for days to go by without my friends and family hearing from me. When the lack of communication would become too great, someone would call or text me to check in and make sure me and KenKay were faring well. The answer was always the same, "we're doing fine. I've just been busy". This was true, aside from the overwhelming feeling of just wanting to be left alone.

I wondered how long it would take me to be able to get past the hurt and pain I was suffering with. I was awaiting the brighter days everyone kept telling me was coming. When I would see Chaun when she visited KenKay the negative emotions would bubble up and I would feel as if any small progress I had made was stolen from me. My patience and tolerance grew short with Chaun. Knowing that she was not having to deal with all the stresses I was faced with day after day was like adding insult to injury. She was now a part time parent and I was left with being the full-time parent alone.

"We have to come up with a schedule that's fair for both of us. The fact that I even have to ask or bring this to you says a lot." I snapped at Chaun one day while she was visiting the twins.

"What do you mean? I told you that I am always available any time you need me." Chaun replied.

"But why should I have to ask?" I barked.

"Because I can't read your mind Candy. And I also can't think you want to see me every day. There is no doubt I want to see my babies every day but we aren't together anymore and I have to respect your space." Chaun said.

"You know how it is. You know how we used to cherish days where we could get a break once in a while. How do you think I feel now that I am doing everything on my own? You are off living your best life and can jump up and do whatever you want, whenever you want."

"Are you kidding me? You think this is living my best life? Not being able to see my kids every day. Not being there when they go to bed or when they wake up. Who would choose that? Who would want that?" she snapped.

"You think I chose this shit either? You think I chose to have a cheating spouse who didn't give two shits about me. Who lied to me and took advantage of me?" I hissed.

"So, Candy this is not really about a schedule for the kids is it? This is still about everything in the past."

"Yeah it may be in the past for you, but it's my every day now."

These hostile interactions were becoming commonplace and I was just over it. I wanted to move on with my life and prayed for God to deliver me from this nightmare I was living. I was slowly getting to the point where I despised Chaun and it seemed like things were getting progressively worse rather than improving. The way things were going solidified for me that I made the right decision.

"I get it Candy. I understand. I am not trying to abandon my responsibility. I know I hurt you and betrayed you but I just pray that one day you can see some sense of good in me again." Chaun said as she was leaving with KenKay.

"I guess only time will tell." I responded as I kissed the twins goodbye. "You two be good. I love you."

"We love you more mommy!" they said in unison.

"You can't avoid the inevitable. Embrace the darkness to appreciate the light. Endure the unhappiness to gain the joy."

- Candy

CHAPTER

Fourteen

The Reunion

*J*alisa and I had gotten into the habit of only checking in with one another once or twice a year. It was not on purpose at all, but we were both living our lives on opposite sides of the country. We had not seen each other since that faithful night at the comedy show when Tamia was reintroduced into my life and it completely got turned upside down. My phone vibrated and I opened it to read the incoming message.

Hey baby! I'm coming to Illinois in a couple of days and I HAVE to see you! It's been way too long.

I smiled when I saw Jalisa's message. For a moment I contemplated giving some excuse why I could not see her because I had been so withdrawn from everybody. But perhaps a little girl's night was just what the doctor ordered to help me alleviate some stress and just be able to let my proverbial hair down for a change. It had been a pretty rough couple of months. I tapped the screen to type my reply.

I would love to see you. Let me know when you will be here and I will have Chaun watch KenKay so you and I can hang out.

Jalisa quickly responded.

It's a date! I can't wait to see you!

I reached out to Chaun and let her know Jalisa was coming to town. She was happy to watch the twins for me so I could reconnect with Jalisa again.

"How is she doing?" Chaun asked.

"She seems to be doing really well from the times I've talked to her before. But you know when we get together she is going to fill me in on everything." I replied.

"Yeah I know. Well tell her I said hello and I hate that I am going to miss her."

"I definitely will."

Jalisa and I solidified our plans and I met her at her mom's house. Jalisa really had no idea the extent of everything that had happened since the comedy show three years ago. I was unsure of the depth I wanted to go with the details but I knew once I told her that Chaun and I were no longer together she was going to want to know what happened. And Jalisa was not the type to accept the generic "it just didn't work out" explanation.

After Jalisa filled me in on how she moved, her new career, her new love interest, and how her daughter was flourishing, the infamous question was posed.

"How are you, Chaun, and the kids doing? I know the last time we talked everything was going so well since the divorce." Jalisa stated.

I paused for a moment and decided I was ready to divulge things to her. She was one of my closest friends and knew just about everything about me anyway. Besides, she was one of my most important support systems when I went through everything with Nicole in college.

"We're not together anymore." I said solemnly.

"Until next week. You guys are a mess. What happened now?" she said jokingly.

Jalisa stopped when she saw I was not laughing with her. I think she knew this time must be different.

"No. This is it for real this time. She doesn't even live with me anymore." I said.

"She moved out?" Jalisa exclaimed.

"Yes. As is everything is gone."

"Oh my goodness. Candy I'm so sorry. Are you ok?" Jalisa said sweetly.

"I am. It had to happen. There had just been too much damage done. She destroyed me J. Like I never knew that level of betrayal before. She did everything Nicole did to me and more."

"Shut up! She slept with someone in your house?" Jalisa exclaimed.

"No. But that was probably the only thing she didn't do." I responded.

Over the next several hours Jalisa and I talked. I brought her up to date on everything that had happened. I told her about how Chaun had ignored my pleads for attention and intimacy. How that lead me to my affairs with Nya and Tamia. I explained to her how I learned of her infidelities, the lies about money and other things, and everything else that had occurred. Jalisa listened on in disbelief.

"I can't believe that Candy. Chaun was so sweet. Like I truly believed she was the best for you. I am so sorry. I understand what lead you here." Jalisa said as she hugged me.

"I don't think anyone could believe it. She put up a good façade. She wears her masks well. She claims she has changed but I don't believe it and I am not going to invest any more time to be the test dummy to find out." I said.

"I can't believe I did not know about you and Tamia. I am going to get her! She kept that under wraps for sure." Jalisa said.

"Don't say anything. It's all in the past now. No need to resurrect something that is dead and gone."

"It's actually funny you say that. Now things kind of make a little more sense to me." she said with a look on her face as if she had just had an epiphany.

"What do you mean?"

"Well, Tamia is still single to this day. She went through a period where she was kind of withdrawn and she just seemed different to me. Maybe there is a reason why she never met anyone that she wanted to date." Jalisa said with a wink.

I sat there in shock for a moment. I had worked so hard over the last almost three years to get over Tamia and the truth of the matter was I never had. I still loved her but had made it up in my mind that she was happily involved with someone and maybe even married by now. After all, it had been years. Did this mean something or nothing at all?

"That doesn't mean anything. Tamia just knew what she wanted and wasn't going to settle for anything less. I could see why she would still be single." I said as I snapped out of my thoughts.

"If you say so. But I am big on all things happening for a reason and nothing really happening by happenstance." Jalisa retorted.

That girl's night with Jalisa sent my mind into a tailspin. It awakened feelings I had buried deep down inside and learned to ignore. There were so many thoughts going through my mind now. I needed to go to my thinking place. The following weekend I took the drive to Chicago and parked my car at the lakefront. I found a rock to sit on where I could see the water splashing and stared out into the horizon. As I sat there watching the waves crash against the rocks, bikers and joggers effortlessly making their way down the paths nearby, I took the time to do some much-needed reflection.

I rarely had time lately to just sit and reflect. I think this was long past due. I realized that it had been two years since my divorce from Chaun and I was still struggling to heal from all the hurt, pain, and disappointment. Everything I had experienced and learned with Chaun's deception had put a deep and long-lasting wound on my heart. I wondered if I would ever be able to love again. It had taken me so long to heal from Nicole and get to the point where I could trust Chaun completely and look where that lead me. Who's to say that would not happen again? Wisdom always told me there was no guarantee when it comes to love but how much hurt and pain can one person endure. And how many gambles do you have to take until you reach the right person that will love you, be honest, and remain loyal to you. For me, it did not seem as if I was asking for too much.

The thing about me is that I love hard and when I invest myself in the relationship, that is all I can see and I expect the same in return. At this point, I literally did not know how to move forward. It was like I was frozen in my tracks and the fear of loving and trusting again was debilitating. I thought back on my past relationships and realized this was the first time since I was fifteen years old that I was completely single. I had jumped from one relationship to the next and I pondered if I was running from something or searching to find something that I had not found. Was I afraid to be alone? Was there a void within myself that I was hoping to fill by having a partner to fill it?

As the sun began to set the purple, red, and orange hues filled the horizon. It was beautiful and serene which was the exact opposite of the tumultuous state of my mind. I realized I had more questions than I had answers but I longed for answers. I craved a sense of peace because I had been living without it for nine years. When I put it into perspective it was disheartening to know the last time I remember having peace was when I proposed to Chaun. After that, it was nonstop with stress and worries from a multitude of sources. How was I going to regain the peace I needed to be able to move on and be made whole again?

I realized I was free from Chaun and Tamia but I was still tied to both. With Chaun we were tied to one another because of the kids, Candy & Chaun, and business. Then Jalisa made me realize I was still tied with Tamia. After all this time, she still had my heart, and she had no idea. The sky was turning dark and I needed to make my way home. I climbed down off the rocks and walked back to my car. After getting in and closing the door, I sat there. That "what if" feeling came over me. It pulled on me and I could not ignore it. I grabbed my cell phone and tapped the little green icon with the phone in it. I found the keypad and stared at it for a moment. Today people rarely commit phone numbers to memory because they are always saved in your cell phone. But there were some that stayed in my mind due to their importance or the necessity for me to have to remember them because of circumstances. I hovered my thumb over the numbers working to recall this number from memory because the pattern would make it familiar again. After doing that a few times, there it was. I took several deep breaths and pushed the green button to send the number over the airwaves and through the various cell towers to connect to the owner of that number. After the third ring I almost hung up and then it happened.

"Hello." the voice on the other end said.

I instantly got butterflies in my stomach. I took another deep breath and could barely speak.

"Hello." the voice said again

"Hello. Can I speak to Tamia?" I asked rhetorically. I already knew it was her because I recognized her voice immediately.

"This is she."

"This is Candy." I said.

"I know. I recognized your number before I answered. How have you been?"

"I've been good. I miss you."

"I miss you too."

"Flexibility in life is imperative. Things will rarely flow as you planned, but what is planned for you will flow."

- Candy

When I made the decision to write this book, I only had the goal of telling my story. I believed by letting people into my background and what I had been through it would help some of those who read it to better understand the woman I am today. I also wanted to let others know they are not alone in the things they have experienced. Life is going to be full of experiences and we will view some of them as positive and others we will view as negative. As I have made it through my life experiences, a lot of them I have shared with you here, I realize there are always lessons that will be learned from them all. The interesting part is that sometimes you do not even gain the lesson or realize what it was until years later. I have even learned more lessons as I put the words on the pages of this book.

So as much as I thought this book was going to be for those that will read it. I realized that maybe this book was more for me. I had prayed for a way to be able to heal from my hurts and this may have been my prayer being answered. I had run from and refused to deal with so much hurt and pain I had experienced and this forced me to relive it. It forced me to look at things a little bit deeper. It forced me to accept some truths I probably would have otherwise ignored. It also made me look at myself and others around me differently.

Sitting down and writing this book was a huge testament to my courage and I gained more to make some difficult decisions that I was probably afraid to make. As emotional as it was to create *Moments of Redemption*, I would not have wanted it any other way. There is one thing that Chaun always said when she did her coaching moments or worked with her clients. She would always say, "You have to deal in order to heal". For me, I believe writing this book was my way of dealing so I could be on my road to healing.

I do not really know what my future holds but I do know that I will work hard to utilize the lessons that I have learned in order to make better decisions and increase the chances of me reaching my ultimate happiness. When I thumb through the pages of this book, I used to ask myself, "why me?" but now I say, "why not me?". Without the things I experienced I may not have realized the level of strength I possess. I may not have been able to recognize the good when it comes my way without having dealt with the bad. I also like to believe that I helped others along the way learn their own lessons and perhaps helped to make them better.

In addition to the entertainment value of this, I hope everyone who chooses to read this will find something that will be able to help you deal with things you may have been unwilling or afraid to deal with. Remember you are stronger, smarter, and more determined than you ever thought you were. You must be willing to tap into those parts of you that seem dark, scary, and even intimidating at times. Those places are what give you the ability to overcome even the worse of situations. As I conclude this, I walk away with this being my moment of redemption and with the strength and readiness to tackle the next set of experiences and receive my next round of lessons that will continue to elevate me to the next level.

THE BEST IS YET TO COME!

About the Author

The author, Candy Johnson, never saw herself as an author. But she noticed when she would share certain aspects of her life, people would always tell her how they were inspired or that something she shared helped them. She gained the courage to write Moments of Redemption and found that it was a source of healing for her.

In writing this book she hoped it would provide a glimpse into how she became the woman she is today. She also wanted others to know they are not alone in the things they have experienced. Yet, as she wrote this book, it became therapeutic and helped her to begin a major healing process in her own life.

In addition to having her master's in business administration, being a mother to twins, entrepreneur, and a motivational speaker, she is honored to add author to her credentials.

Connect with Candy Johnson:

Facebook: Candy Sincerity Johnson

Instagram: candysincerityjohnson

Made in USA - Crawfordsville, IN
65733_9781089301240
08.08.2023 1804